TOTAL QUALITY MANAGEMENT

AF517342

TOTAL QUALITY MANAGEMENT

By

Mr. G. Murugesan
Asst. Professor
Deptt. of Management Studies
V.M.K.V. Engineering College
Salem
Tamil Nadu

UNIVERSITY SCIENCE PRESS

(An Imprint of Laxmi Publications Pvt. Ltd.)

BANGALORE • CHENNAI • COCHIN • GUWAHATI • HYDERABAD
JALANDHAR • KOLKATA • LUCKNOW • MUMBAI • RANCHI
NEW DELHI

Published by :
UNIVERSITY SCIENCE PRESS
(*An Imprint of Laxmi Publications Pvt. Ltd.*)
113, Golden House, Daryaganj,
New Delhi-110002
Phone : 011-43 53 25 00
Fax : 011-43 53 25 28
www.laxmipublications.com
info@laxmipublications.com

Copyright © 2011 by Laxmi Publications Pvt. Ltd. All rights reserved. No part of this publication may be reproduced, stored in a retrieval system, or transmitted in any form or by any means, electronic, mechanical, photocopying, recording or otherwise without the prior written permission of the publisher.

First Edition : 2011

OFFICES

✆ **Bangalore**	080-26 61 15 61	✆ **Jalandhar**	0181-222 12 72
✆ **Chennai**	044-24 34 47 26	✆ **Kolkata**	033-22 27 43 84
✆ **Cochin**	0484-237 70 04, 405 13 03	✆ **Lucknow**	0522-220 95 78
✆ **Guwahati**	0361-254 36 69, 251 38 81	✆ **Mumbai**	022-24 91 54 15, 24 92 78 69
✆ **Hyderabad**	040-24 65 23 33	✆ **Ranchi**	0651-221 47 64

UTQ-955-4-090-TOTAL QUALITY MANAG-MUR C—
Typeset at : Goswami Associates, Delhi.

CONTENTS

SYLLABUS

UNIT I: INTRODUCTION

Definition of quality - Dimensions of quality, quality planning, quality costs - Analysis techniques for quality costs, Basic concepts of TQM, Historical review, principles of TQM, Leadership concepts, Role of senior Management, quality council, quality statements, strategic planning, Deming philosophy, Barriers to TQM implementation.

UNIT II: TQM PRINCIPLES

Customer satisfaction - Customer perception of quality, Customer complaints, Service quality, Customer retention, Employee involvement - Motivation, Empowerment, Teams, Recognition and Reward , Performance Appraisal, Benefits, Continuous Process Improvement - Juran Trilogy, PDSA cycle, 5S, Kaizen, Supplier Partnership - Partnering, Sourcing, Supplier selection, Supplier rating ,Relation ship development, Performance Measures-Basic concepts, Strategy, performance measure.

UNIT III: STATISTICAL PROCESS CONTROL

The seven tools of quality, statistical fundamentals - Measures of central tendency and dispersion, population and sample, normal curve, control charts for variables and attributes, process capability, concept of six sigma, new seven management tools.

UNIT IV: TQM TOOLS

Benchmarking – Reasons to Benchmark, Benchmarking Process, Quality Function Deployment (QFD) – House of Quality, QFD Process, Benefits, Taguchi Quality Loss Function, Total Productive Maintenance (TPM) – Concept, Improvement Needs, FMEA – Stages of FMEA.

UNIT - V: QUALITY SYSTEMS

Needs for ISO 9000 and other quality systems, ISO 9000: 2000 quality system - Elements, Implementation of quality system, Documentation, quality auditing, QS 9000, ISO 14000 - concepts, requirements and benefits.

PREFACE

It is indeed a great pleasure and proud privilege for me to present this treatise on 'Total Quality Management' to the immediate benefit of final year engineering students of all branches. This book is written in tune with the latest syllabus of various universities and we have taken the syllabus as guidelines for the organization of this book.

In writing this book, the author has constantly kept in mind the tremendous amount of ground which the student and the practicing engineers of today is expected to cover. No effort has been spared to enrich the book with simple language and self-explanatory diagrams.

The author's responsibility here is to stress abundantly that we lay on no chaim to the original research in preparing this text. Many of the subject matters that are available in the works of eminent authors have been made freely. Perhaps, what we may chaim, in all modesty, is that we have tried to fashion the vast amount of materials available from primary and secondary sources into coherent body of description and analysis.

I am very thankful to Dr. A. Shanmugasundram, Chancellor of Vinayaka Missions Unversity, Salem, Tamil Nadu. Dr. A. Nagappan, Principal, Prof. P. Ganasekaran, Dean, Placement, V.M.K.V. Engineering College, Periya Seeragapadi, Salem, Tamil Nadu. It's my great pleasure to express may heartfelt gratitude to my wife and my daughter who have shouldered my burdens for the successful completion of my book.

—Author

Unit 1 INTRODUCTION

1.1 MEANING OF QUALITY

Quality refers to the end-use of the product. Quality is the requirement of customers.

For example, the gear used in the sugarcane juice extracting machine may not possess good surface finish, tolerance and accuracy as compared with one used in the headstock of a lathe.

1.2 DEFINITION OF QUALITY

"Quality is the totality of features and characteristics of a product or service at bear on its ability to satisfy stated or implied needs". **—ISO 8402**

"Quality is fitness for use". **—Juran**

"Quality is a predictable degree of uniformity and dependability at low cost and suited to the market". **—Deming**

1.3 DIMENSIONS OF QUALITY

Quality has nine different dimensions. These are explained under the table.

Sl. No.	Dimensions	Meaning	Examples
1.	**Performance**	Primary operating characteristics of a product.	Signal coverage, audio quality, display quality, etc.
2.	**Features**	Secondary characteristics that supplement the product are basic functioning.	Remote control given along with A/C unit or television
3.	**Reliability**	Probability of successful operation within the stipulated time period.	
4.	**Conformance**	Meeting the predetermined standards or specifications.	
5.	**Durability**	It is a measure of product life including economical and technical dimensions	
6.	**Serviceability**	Solution to the complaints given by the customer.	
7.	**Response**	Human to human interface.	Quick response to the customer complaints.
8.	**Aesthetics**	Sensory characteristics	Surface finish, fashion
9.	**Reputation**	Indirect evaluation of quality gained by past performance and other intangibles.	Courtesy, being ranked first and pioneer.

1.4 QUALITY PLANNING

Quality planning attempts to meet the quality needs of the customers. Quality planning involves creating a process that will be able to meet established goals and do so under operating conditions. It is a strategic planning process in which quality is embedded in each and every step.

In order to meet the customer needs, a quality planning road map can be prepared. Following are the steps which are involved in preparing quality planning road map.

- Establish quality goals
- Identify the customers
- Determine the customer needs
- Develop product features which respond to the customer needs
- Develop processes that are able to produce the product features
- Establish the quality controls
- Transfer the plans to operating forces

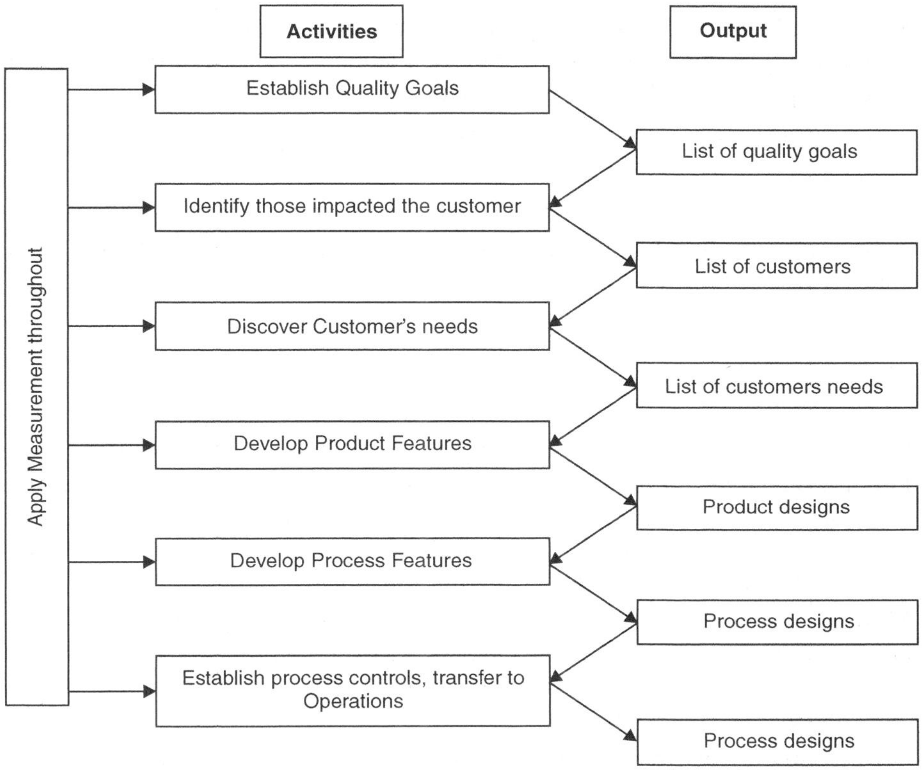

FIGURE 1.1 **Quality Planning Road Map (From Juran, 1990)**

Output of each preceding activity or steps become the input for the next step and so on.

Application of Quality Planning Road Map

It is applicable to all industries in both manufacturing and service sectors. It is applicable at levels in an organization and its all functional areas.

The quality planning road map can be applied at the following levels:

- Supervisory and worker level
- Functional level
- Multifunctional systems
- Major programmes

(*a*) **Supervisory and Workers Level.** Each employee is assigned a large. Large number of jobs requires quality planning as well as re-planning as the job may be dynamic. In some cases the employee themselves are given training to plan their job. The concepts and tools which are used for quality planning at this stage are

- Self-control concept
- Triple role concept.

Self control concept. This concept reveals that the person should have full control as well as mastery over the attainment of the planned results. In order to achieve the self control, a person should be provided with

— *Knowledge of what he is supposed to do*

— *Knowledge of what others are doing*

— *Means for regulating either of the above two, if the failure to meet the objective results.*

Triple role concept. This concept stresses that each employee holding a job should be able to carry out the following three roles

— *As a customer*

— *As a processor*

— *As a supplier*

Using this concept natural progress of quality planning can be achieved.

(*b*) **Functional Level.** Functional managers are the in-charge of different areas. They undertake quality planning to manage their performance in a better position. For example, Production Manager is the in-charge of different areas of his department. He makes a quality planning to expose his performance in a better manner.

(*c*) **Multifunctional System.** Systems such as Management Information System, HR, and New product development system have spread over their functional areas, as they receive inputs from all the major functional areas. So adequate quality planning is required for the betterment of the working systems.

Central quality planning is highly useful in achieving coordination among all the functional areas involved. The central quality planning can be achieved through any one of the following

— A team (or committee) of functional managers

— A team (or committee) of functional managers with the assistance of quality specialist

— A project management department

— A quality assurance department

(*d*) **Major Programmes.** Major programmes is otherwise termed as costly projects such as nuclear power plants, development of new weapon system, launching a satellite into space and so on. These projects are complex and unique. So they require specific quality planning.

In these types of projects/programmes, it is common for clients to specify the quality plans and also the product/project organization requires central quality planning system.

1.5 QUALITY COSTS

Quality cost is the cost, which do not meet the customer requirements. In other words it is the cost of poor products or services.

Quality costs are those costs associated with the non- achievement of products/services.

Elements of Quality Costs

The following are the elements of quality costs:

- Prevention cost
- Appraisal cost
- Internal failure cost
- External failure cost

(*a*) **Prevention cost.** Prevention costs are the costs that are incurred on preventing a quality problem. Prevention cost includes cost of quality planning, documenting, process control, training, preventing defects, investigation analysis and correction of defects etc.

(*b*) **Appraisal cost.** Appraisal costs are the costs that are incurred in assessing that the products/services conformance with the requirements or specifications. It includes the cost of activities viz. inspection all kind of testing designed to find quality problems.

(*c*) **Internal failure cost.** Internal failure costs arise due to internal failures. These costs are associated with correcting the mistakes before delivery of the products. Internal failure cost includes the cost of scrap, rework, failure analysis, re-inspection, re-testing and downgrading.

(*d*) **External failure cost.** External failure costs are associated with the adjustment of defectives after the delivery of the products. This includes service cost, cost of warranty and guarantee claims, customer rejects or complaints, complaint investigation and lost of sales cost due to loss of goodwill, cost of product reliability compensation etc.

1.6 OPTIMUM COST OF PERFORMANCE

The model for optimum quality cost is explained as under.

(*i*) **Failure cost.** It consists of internal and external failure costs. It will be zero, when the product is 100% good. And it will be infinity when the product is 100% defective.

(*ii*) **Appraisal and prevention cost.** This cost is zero when the product is 100% defective and it increases as perfection is approached.

(*iii*) **Total quality cost.** This is the sum of the failure cost and appraisal and prevention cost. The curve represents the total cost per good unit of product. The total quality cost curve is divided into three zones. They are

— Zone of improvement projects

— Zone of high appraisal cost

— Zone of indifference

Zone of improvement projects. This lies in the left side of the curve. In this zone the failure cost occupy more than 70% of the total quality cost and the prevention cost occupy less than 10%. In this case by improving the quality of conformance, the total cost can be reduced.

Zone of high appraisal cost. This lies in the right side of the curve. In this zone, the appraisal cost exceeds the failure cost.

Zone of indifference. This lies in the centre of the curve. In this zone, the failure costs are usually 50% of the total quality cost while the prevention cost are about 10%. The optimum level is achieved by implementing quality improvement projects.

Improving the quality of conformance results in a reduction of total cost which is contrary to the belief of that higher quality results in the higher costs. By moving toward the optimum from either the zone of improvement projects or zone of high appraisal cost, a reduction in cost can be achieved.

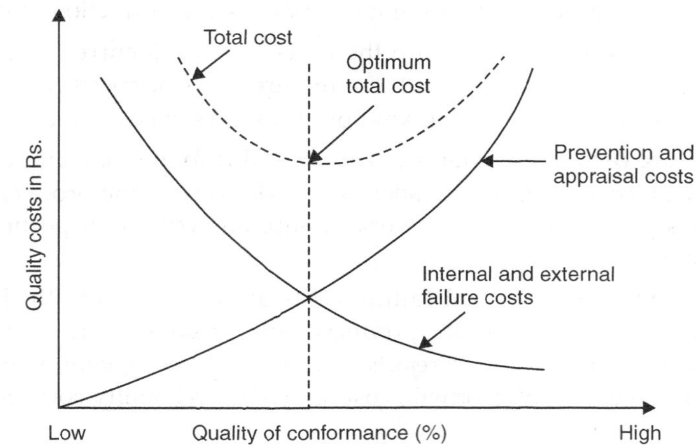

FIGURE 1.2 **Economics of Quality of Conformance**

From the above figure 1.2, we can understand that to achieve a reduction in failure cost, it is necessary to increase prevention and appraisal cost.

Uses of quality cost analysis

- To identify profit opportunities.
- To identify quality problems.
- To improve purchasing and supplier related costs.
- To determine whether the quality cost are properly distributed.
- To establish goal for budgets and profit planning.
- To make capital budgeting and investment decisions.

1.7 ANALYSIS TECHNIQUES FOR QUALITY COSTS

The following techniques are used for analyzing the quality costs:

- Trend Analysis
- Pareto Analysis

The objective of the above techniques is to determine opportunities for quality improvement.

(*a*) **Trend Analysis.** Trend analysis is a tool for plan that provides information for long range planning.

It also provides information for the investigation and assessment of quality improvement programmes. It compares the present quality cost levels to past quality cost levels.

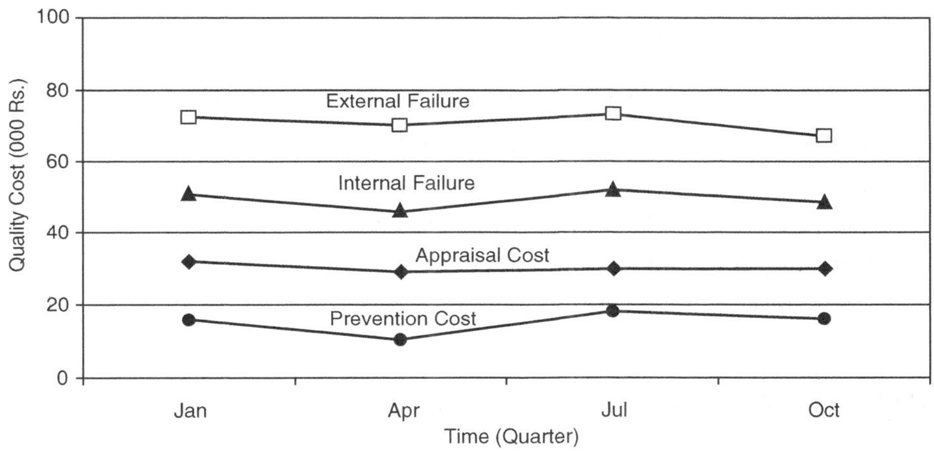

FIGURE 1.3 **Trend Chart**

(*b*) **Pareto Analysis.** Under the Pareto diagram, the data classifications are ranked in descending order from left to right. The "vital few" (important few) are placed on the left and the "trivial many" (many insignificant problems) are in the right. It is sometimes necessary to combine some of the trivial many into one classification called "other" and it is placed on the extreme right.

From the figure 1.4, this Pareto diagram is used to identify the most important problem. In this diagram, 77% of total defectiveness is resulting from first three items (incomplete, surface scars and cracks) only. So these are analyzed intensively. These items are identified by listing them in descending order in the graph which provides a visual impact showing those vital few characteristics that need attention. Thus, the Pareto diagram is a powerful quality improvement tools.

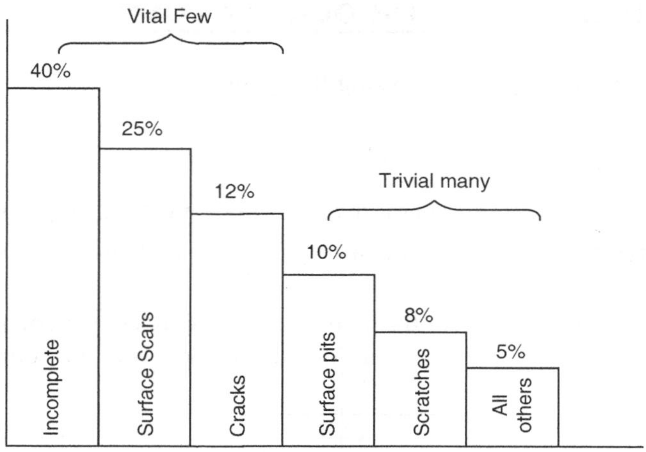

FIGURE 1.4 **Pareto Diagram for Quality Cost by Defectives**

The following are the examples of vital few items:

— A few customers who buy more.

— A few processes which cause for more scrap or rework cost.

— A few non-conformities which led to the major customer complaints.

— A few stock items account for more inventory cost.

1.8 TOTAL QUALITY MANAGEMENT (TQM)

1.8.1 Meaning of TQM

The word TQM is segregated into the following manner.

Total — *Made up of the whole*

Quality — *Degree of excellence of products or services*

Management — *Art or Science of handling, directing, controlling etc.*

In short, TQM is the art of managing the whole to achieve excellence.

TQM is a management philosophy of achieving continuous improvement in functional areas such as marketing, finance, design, engineering, production and customer service etc. through the integrated efforts of all individuals in the organization towards meeting the customer needs and organizational objectives.

1.8.2 Definition of TQM

"TQM is the management approach of an organization centered on quality, based on the participation of all its members and aiming at long time success through customer satisfaction, and benefits to all members of the organizations and to society". **—ISO**

"TQM is the control of all transformation processes of an organization to best satisfy customers needs in the most economical manner". **—Prof. Leopald S.Vasin**

1.8.3 Characteristics of TQM

Following are the characteristics of TQM.

- TQM is a customer oriented.
- TQM required a long term commitment for continuous improvement of all process.
- TQM is a team work.
- TQM requires the commitment of the top level management and continuous involvement.
- TQM is a strategy for continuous improvement of performance at all levels.

1.8.4 Basic Concepts of TQM

A successful TQM programme requires the following six basic concepts:

(*a*) **Top management commitment.** Top management should participate in the total quality programme. They should ensure their complete commitment to the approach through management meetings. The top management should make sure that everybody in the organization is communicated about the TQM.

(*b*) **Focus on the customer.** Customer satisfaction is the life blood of TQM. Customers include both internal and external customers. So focus on the customer is the key for any TQM programme.

(*c*) **Effective involvement and utilization of the entire workforce.** This concept also known as ***"Principle of employees involvement" or "respect for people".*** Total quality recognizes that each person is responsible for the quality of his/her work. All the persons must be trained in TQM.

(*d*) **Continuous improvement.** TQM is based on the quest for progress and improvement. TQM believes that there is always a better way of doing things, way to make better use of the companies total quality resources, a way to be more productive. For this purpose various quality tools and techniques may be used.

(*e*) **Treating suppliers as partners.** Since the suppliers influence the company's quality, therefore a partnering relationship should be developed between the management and suppliers.

(*f*) **Establishing performance measures for the processes.** Quantitative data are necessary to measure the continuous quality improvement. Therefore performance measures such as productivity, sales turnover, time management, absenteeism, customer satisfaction etc. should be determined for each functional area. These results can be used for further improvement.

1.8.5 Elements of TQM

Following are the elements of TQM.

(*a*) **The philosophical elements.** The philosophical elements of TQM stress the operation of the company using quality as the integrating element.

(*b*) **The generic tools.** The generic tools consist of various statistical process control methods that are used for problem solving and continuous improvement.

(*c*) **Tools of the quality control departments.** It consists of statistical quality control methods such as sampling plans, process capability, and Taguchi methods.

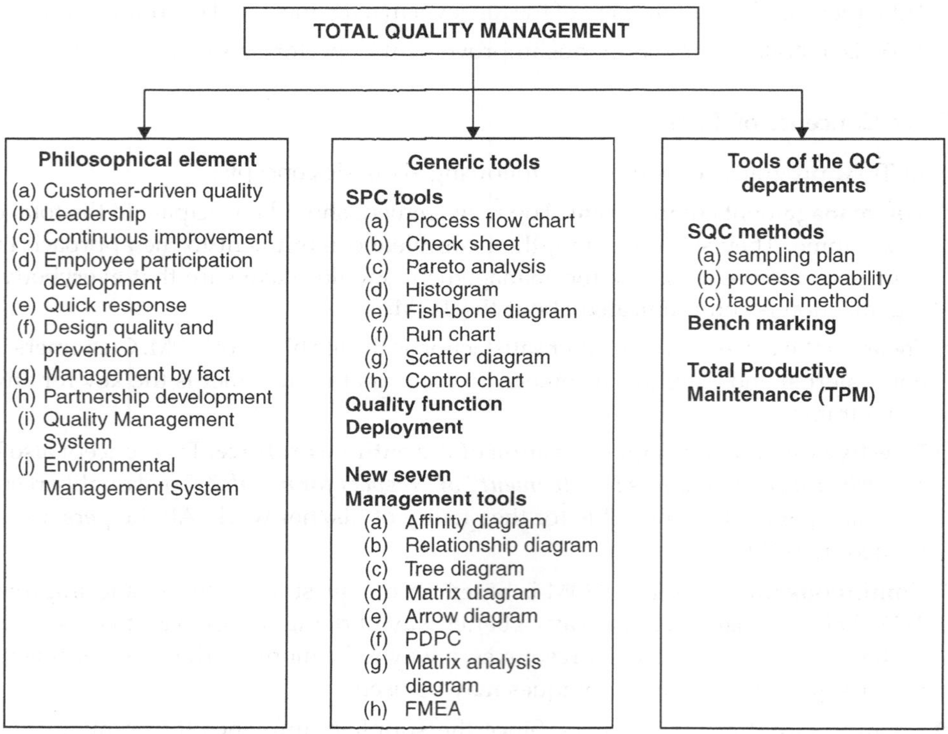

FIGURE 1.5 **Elements of TQM**

1.8.6 Pillars of TQM

There are four pillars of TQM.

- Problem solving discipline
- Interpersonal skills
- Teamwork
- Quality improvement process.

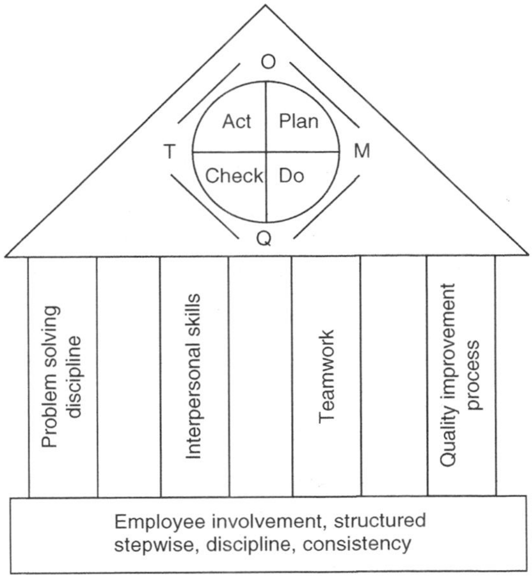

FIGURE 1.6 **TQM House with Pillars**

TQM is used to improve the whole organization stepwise, structured and systematically according to hard work, discipline, intensive training and consistent implementation of techniques and resources.

1.8.7 Historical Review of TQM

Period	Events
Prior to the 20th century	Quality is an art. Demands over potential production an era of workmanship
F.W. Taylor 1900s	Scientific approach to management resulting in rationalization of work and its breakdown leads to greater need for standardization, inspection and supervision.
Shewart 1930s	Statistical beginning and the study of quality control. In parallel, studies by R.A.Fisher on experimental design. The beginning of control charts at Western Electric in USA
Late 1930s	Quality standards and approaches are introduced in France and Japan Beginning of SQC, reliability and maintenance engineering
1942	Seminar work by Deming at the Ministry of War in USA on quality control and sampling. Working group set up by Juran and Dodge on SQC in US army. Concepts of acceptance sampling devised
1944	Dodge and Deming carried out seminar research on acceptance sampling
1945	Founding of the Japan Standard Association

1946	Founding of the American Society for Quality Control (ASQC)
1951	Quality Assurance accepted
1954	TQC in Japan (Feigenbaum & Juran) book published 1956
1957	Founding of European organization for the control of quality
1961	The Martin company in USA introduced the zero defects approach, while developing and producing pershing missiles (Crosby). Quality motivation started in USA and integrated programmes were begun
1962	Quality circle were started in Japan
1964	Ishikawa published book on Quality Management
1970	Ishikawa published book on Quality Circles and the concept of TQM was affirmed and devised in Japanese industries.
1970 - 1980	JIT and quality became crucial for competitiveness. A large number of US and European corporations were started to appreciate the advance of Japanese industries. Taguchi popularize the use of environmental designs and products.
1980 - 1990	Facing the rising sun challenge in quality management. Development and introduction of FMS's and greater dependence on supplier contracts. Growth of economic based on quality control and information software packages.
1990 onwards	The management of quality has become a necessity that is recognized at all levels of management. Increasing importance is given to off-line quality management for the design of robust manufacturing processes and products. The growth of process optimization.

1.8.8 Principles of TQM

Following are the important principles of TQM.

(*a*) Customer's requirements must be met always.

(*b*) There must be agreed requirements for both internal and external customers.

(*c*) All levels of management people must be involved effectively in all functional areas.

(*d*) Regular two way communication (both formal and informal) with staff at all level is must.

(*e*) Identification of training needs and individual capacities are must.

(*f*) Top level management's participation is must.

(*g*) A culture of continuous improvement must be established.

(*h*) Importance should be given to the purchasing and supplier management.

(*i*) Every job must add value.

(*j*) Quality improvement must eliminate waste and reduce the total cost.

(*k*) There must be a focus on the prevention of problems.

(*l*) A culture of promoting creativity must be established.

(*m*) Performance measures are must at organization, departments, and individual levels. It helps to assess and meet objectives of quality.

(*n*) There should be focus on team work.

1.8.9 Barriers (Obstacles) to TQM Implementation

(*a*) Lack of management commitment.

(*b*) Lack of faith in and support to TQM activities among management personnel.

(*c*) Inability to change organizational culture.

(*d*) Misunderstanding about TQM concepts.

(*e*) Improper planning.

(*f*) Lack of employee's commitment.

(*g*) Lack of effective communication.

(*h*) Lack of continuous training and education.

(*i*) Lack of interest or incompetence of leaders.

(*j*) Ineffective measurement techniques and lack of assess to data and results.

(*k*) Non-application of proper tools and techniques.

(*l*) Inadequate use of empowerment and team work.

(*m*) Inadequate attention to internal and external customers.

(*n*) Delay or non-implementation of quality improvement team's recommendations.

1.8.10 Benefits of TQM

The benefits of TQM are classified into two categories viz. (*a*) Tangible and (*b*) Intangible.

(*a*) **Tangible benefits**

- Improved product quality
- improved productivity
- Reduced quality cost
- Increased market and customers
- Increased profitability
- Reduced employee grievances

(*b*) **Intangible benefits**

- Improved employee participation
- Improved team work
- Improved customer satisfaction
- Improved working relationship
- Improved communication

- Enhancement of the job interest
- Enhanced problem solving capacity
- Improved company good will

1.9 LEADERSHIP

1.9.1 Definition

"Leadership is the ability to do inspire people positively to make a total, willing and voluntary commitment to accomplish the organizational goals". **—TQM**

"Leadership is we, not me; mission, not my show; vision, not division; and community, not domicile".

—Rick L. Edgeman

1.9.2 Characteristics of Quality Leader

(*a*) They give primary attention to external and internal customers and their needs.
(*b*) They have empowerment rather than controlling their subordinates.
(*c*) They give emphasis to improvement rather than maintenance.
(*d*) They give priority to prevention.
(*e*) They encourage collaboration rather than competition.
(*f*) They train and coach rather than direct and supervise.
(*g*) They learn from problems.
(*h*) They are trying to improve the communication skills continually.
(*i*) They demonstrate their commitment to quality.
(*j*) They choose their supplier on the basis of quality but not on price.
(*k*) They establish the organizational system to improve the quality.
(*l*) They encourage and recognize the team effort.

1.9.3 Difference between Leader and Manager

Leaders	Managers
Leaders create energy by inspiring.	Managers control and direct energy.
Leaders do the right things.	Managers do things right.
Leaders are essential for the group.	Managers are necessary in an organization.

1.9.4 Habits of Quality Leaders

Following are the habits of quality leaders:

- Being a proactive than reactive in nature
- Beginning with the end in mind
- Putting first things first
- Thinking win-win
- Seeking first to understand, then to be understood
- Gathering people together for teamwork
- Sharpen the saw (Renewing)

(*i*) **Being a proactive than reactive in nature.** Being proactive means taking responsibility for one self. Reactive people let circumstances, conditions or their environment tells them how to respond. Proactive people think carefully think and respond.

Comparisons between reactive and proactive behaviours are given below:

Proactive	Reactive
I will do by using alternative method	I can't do anything
I control my feelings send her out	She disturbed me a lot
I want to do it	I have to do that
I can	I can't
I prefer	I must
I make things better	The things are getting worse.

(*ii*) **Beginning with the end in mind.** Begin each day with an imagination as the end of your life as the frame of reference. All things are created twice - first as mental creation (imagination). Second as physical creation. Plan is a first creation of a building. Actual building is a second physical creation. To have a successful organization, you should begin with a plan that will produce the appropriate end.

(*iii*) **Putting first things first.** This habit makes the leader manage time precisely. It means self-management and requires first two habits as prerequisites. Time management matrix should be diagrammed for accomplishing day by day, movement by movement management of time.

(*iv*) **Thinking win-win.** Think always positively. To obtain win-win, a four step process is required.

(*a*) View the problem from the other viewpoint

(*b*) Identify the key issues and concerns

(*c*) Determine acceptable results

(*d*) Seek possible new options to achieve those results.

(*v*) **Seeking first to understand, then to be understood.** Listening is the key to effective communication. It makes you know how other person sees the world and how they feel. Listening means not that you agree with someone. It means that fully, deeply understand that person emotionally as well as intellectually. Next is—to be understood, to be affirmed, to be validated and to be appreciated.

(*vi*) **Gathering people together for teamwork.** The unity is greater than the parts. Build on the positive quality of others and ignore their bad qualities. Teamwork is a powerful weapon for effectiveness.

(*vii*) **Sharpen the saw (Renewing).** Take time to sharpen the saw so it will cut faster. It is personal PC-preserving and enhancing the greatest asset you have, which you is. It is renewing the four dimensions of your nature-physical, spiritual, mental and social or emotional. All four dimensions of your nature must be used regularly in wise and balanced ways.

1.9.5 Leadership Concepts

Effective leadership requires understanding about the human nature (*i.e.*, basic requirements). A successful leader must know the talents of his subordinates. The following are very important for an effective leadership

- People need security (job and life) and independence (decision-making and execution) at the same time.
- People get self-motivated when they become involved in their work. External rewards and punishments can also enhance the motivation of the people.
- People like to be praised by others. So the leaders should find every opportunity to praise their employees. This will improve the morale.
- Since people can process and execute only few facts at a time, a leader should simply the tasks.
- People like to work based on their gut feeling rather than the statistical data.
- People will not respect a leader if the leader does not act according to his words.

1.9.6 Leadership Role

Effective team work requires effective leaders. Effective leaders are people who can perform different roles. Quinn lists the following eight roles.

(*a*) **Producer role**

- Promotes a productive working environment
- Commands great involvement and personal dedication
- Time/stress management

(*b*) **Director role**

- Develops policy and rules
- Formulates plans
- Identifies bottlenecks

(*c*) **Coordinator role**

- Organize and coordinates efforts of personnel
- Focused on delegation of tasks
- Pays attention to technological issues

(*d*) **Checker role**

- Watches over and guides achievements
- Takes care of details and documentation
- Checks if people stick to the rules.

(*e*) **Stimulator role**

- Realize teamwork
- Participatory decision–making
- Reaches consensus
- Openness, involvement and solidarity

(*f*) **Mentor role**

- Develops skills of people
- Has a careful, helpful and systematic approach
- Gives compliments and honour to the achiever

(*g*) **Innovator role**

- Makes continuous improvements possible
- Has a vision of the future
- Recognizes importance trends
- Anticipates changes

(*h*) **Negotiator**

- Uses power and influences people
- Can negotiate effectively
- Have image, reputation, and pervasive power.

1.10 ROLE OF SENIOR MANAGEMENT

Important role of senior management are listed below.

(*a*) **Establish quality policies.** The top management should establish quality council policies related to TQM. The senior managers should establish a quality council to improve the quality culture in the organization.

(*b*) **Develop a leadership system.** Senior management should develop a leadership system at all levels in all functions of the organization including manufacturing, marketing, research, sales, finance, and human resources. Senior managers should provide the skills to implement quality control techniques and active participation in the quality council.

(*c*) **Management by wandering around (MBWA).** Senior management should get out of the office and visit customers, suppliers, and departments with in the organization. This will help the managers to know what is happening around them. This technique reduces the paper works, encourages the subordinates, and is used to get the first hand information. Speaking face-to-face with workforce will improve the involvement of employees in achieving the organization goals.

(*d*) **Strategy of decision making and problem solving.** Senior management alone cannot take a final decision, but to make sure the team's decision is aligned with the quality statements of the organization. By delegating authority and responsibility, the problem solving and decision making works are carried out at all levels of the organization.

(*e*) **Strong information base.** Senior managers should update their knowledge on quality improvement by reading books and articles, attending seminars and workshops, and talking to other TQM leaders.

(*f*) **Provide the resources to train the employees.** The management should provide the necessary resources to train the employees in TQM tools and techniques, the technical requirements of the job, and safety. Resources in the form of appropriate equipments to do the job should also be provided.

(*g*) **Award and recognition.** Senior management should celebrate the success of their organization's quality efforts by personality participating in award and recognition functions. Quality council should be formed to establish or revise the recognition and reward system and also to revise the senior management incentive compensation system.

(*h*) **Spend more time on quality.** Senior managers should be visibly and actively engaged in the quality effort by coaching and serving on teams, and teaching seminars. They should demonstrate, communicate and reinforce the quality statements. Ultimately, the senior managers should spend atleast one-third of their time on quality.

(*i*) **Effective communication.** Senior management should create awareness of the importance of TQM and to communicate the results of TQM to every one in the organization.

(*j*) **Identify and encourage potential employees.** Every person has some talents and potentials in nature. Senior managers should identify and explore these talented employees to use their talent towards TQM efforts.

(*k*) **Responsibility on quality.** The senior managers are also responsible for the quality of output from the work area. They should accept the responsibility and accountability for the output from their own areas and investigate causes for it and formulate action plans for improvement.

(*l*) **Role model.** Each manager is responsible to set the standards for quality through their own actions and behaviour. The management can expect a total commitment to quality from employees only if the management follows principles proposed by them. Because, the employees always watch the activities of the management. Thus, the steps taken by the senior management to improve the quality should be revealed to every employee in the organization.

(*m*) **Minimize the resistance to change.** Since TQM requires a total change, resistance may arise from different levels in an organization. The employees may feel about their job security, loss of authority, increased work load, doubt about top management commitment etc. Therefore, the top management should try to minimize the resistance to change, break down barriers, and remove system road blocks and to remove the fear about the organization.

(*n*) **Listening internal and external customers and suppliers.** It is a very important role of senior managers to listen the internal and external customers and suppliers through visits, focus groups, and surveys. This, information is translated into core values and process improvement projects.

(*o*) The senior managers should periodically check whether the quality improvement programs are conducted as per the plan.

To summarize, senior management should develop the strategy for quality and assures its implementation through personal leadership.

1.11 QUALITY COUNCIL

A quality council is established to provide over all direction. It is the driver for the TQM engine. It develops the quality strategy and guide and supports their implementations. The quality council is consisting of Chief Executive Officer (CEO); and the senior managers of the functional areas such as Marketing, Finance, Production and Quality; and coordinator or consultant. If there is a union, union representative is also given membership in the quality council. Some organization includes their front-line representatives from each area.

Duties of the Quality Council

- Developing the core values and quality statements. Quality statements include Vision, Mission, Quality policy statements.
- Developing the strategic planning with goals and annual quality improvement program with objectives.
- To create education and training programme.
- To determine and monitor the cost of poor quality continuously.
- To determine the performance for the organization, approve the functional areas.
- To determine those projects that improve the process continuously, that affects the internal and external customer satisfaction.
- To establish the multi-functional projects and departmental work and monitor their progress.
- To establish/revise the recognition and reward system periodically.

Once the TQM program is well established, a typical agenda might have the following items:

- Progress report on teams
- Customer satisfaction report
- New project teams

- Recognition dinner
- Benchmarking report.

1.12 QUALITY STATEMENTS

The quality statements include

- Vision statement,
- Mission statement and
- Quality policy statement.

1.12.1 Vision Statement

The vision statement is a declaration of what an organization aims to be tomorrow. It is the ideal state which we should strive continuously to achieve. The vision statement provides a guidelines for decision-making.

For example, the vision statement of Vinayaka Mission's is as follows

"To achieve excellence in education. To make education, a tool for social change for the betterment of the society."

The Vision statement of All India Council for Technical Education (AICTE) is given below.

"To be a world class organization, leading technological and socio-economic development of the country by enhancing the global competitiveness of technical manpower and by ensuring high quality technical education to all sections of the society".

1.12.2 Mission Statement

Mission statement is the function of the organization. It provides the clear statement of purpose for employees, customers and suppliers. The mission statement answers the following questions:

Who we are?

Who are the customers?

What we do?

How we do it?

For example, eliminating poverty is the mission of Indian Government.

The Mission statement of Vinayaka Mission's is as follows:

"To spread education globally in the field of Medicine, Dental, Paramedical, Homoeopathy, Engineering, Management and basic science using existing resources and technology".

1.12.3 Quality Policy Statement

Quality policy is a guide for everyone in the organization as to have they provide products and services to the customers. It should be written by the CEO with feedback from the workforce and be approved by the quality council. It is an important requirement of ISO 9000 quality systems.

For example, ISO 9000 Quality policy of V.M.K.V. Engineering College, Salem is as follows:

- ***To make the students exposed to the latest engineering and technological advancement***
- ***To make the students prepared with knowledge, skill and competence to stand up to any challenges in the spheres of Engineering, Science, Technology and Management***
- ***To make our college an institution of excellence internationally and improve continually to match the needs of the production and services sectors, and society.***

Characteristics of quality policy

- *Quality is the first priority.*
- *Internal and external customer's needs should be fulfilled.*
- *Exceed or atleast equal to the competitors products or services.*
- *Continuous quality improvement is essential.*
- *Utilization of entire resources of organization.*
- *Include business and production processes.*

1.13 STRATEGIC PLANNING

Strategy means a direction, guide, or course of action. Strategic planning is a process by which organizations develop a vision, mission, objectives and goals for its achievement. It is the highest level of managerial activity, usually performed by the company's CEO and executive team. Strategic planning process determines strategic advantages to the business environment the organization faces. The time horizon for strategic planning is three to ten years. So, it is called as long term planning.

1.13.1 Strategic Planning Process

There are seven basic steps for strategic quality planning. They are explained as under.

(*a*) **Customer needs.** It is the first step is the identification of customers and their wants and needs. An organization must seek its customer's requirements, expectations and assess future trends before developing a strategic plan.

(*b*) **Customer positioning.** The planners determine where the organization wants to be in relation to the customers. Do they want to retain, reduce, or expand the customer base? The organization needs to concentrate its efforts on areas of excellence. Products or services with poor quality performance should be eliminated.

(*c*) **Predict the future.** The planners must predict future conditions that will affect the products or services. To help predicting the future, the tools such as demographics, economic forecast and technical assessment or projections may be used.

(*d*) **Gap analysis.** The planners should identify the gaps between the current state and the future state of the organization. An analysis of the core values and concepts is an excellent technique for pinpointing the gaps.

(*e*) **Closing the gap.** The planners should develop a plan to close the gap by establishing goals and responsibilities. All stockholders should be involved in the development of the plan.

(*f*) **Alignment.** As the plan is developed it must be aligned with the mission, vision and core values and concepts of the organizations. Without this alignment, the plan will have little chance of success.

(*g*) **Implementation.** The last step in strategic planning process is implementation which is more frequently the difficult one. Resources must be allocated to collecting data, designing changes and overcoming resistance to change. Also part of this step is the monitoring activity to ensure that progress is being made. The planning group should meet atleast once in a year to assess progress and take any corrective actions.

1.14 DEMING PHILOSOPHY

Dr. W. Edward Deming is called as the ***"Father of Japanese Quality Revolution"***. He has approached the quality management problem from a statistician's perspective. He proposed 14 points on route to quality through the use of statistical techniques. Most of these points were given in a seminar for 21 presidents of leading Japanese industry in 1950. The rest were developed and the original once modified over a period of three decades. Deming defines quality in terms of quality of design, quality of conformance and quality of the sales and service functions. The 14 principles are explained as under.

(*a*) **Create and publish the aims and purpose of the organization.** Create and publish the aims and purposes of the organization to all employees and other organizations. Establish the continuous improvement of products or services in order to become competitive, stay in business and provide jobs to employees.

(*b*) **Learn the new philosophy.** Adopt the new philosophy of rejecting of poor workmanship, defective products, or bad services. The organization must concentrate on defect prevention rather than defect deduction. Every one in the organization must be involved in the quality improvement.

(*c*) **Understand the purpose of inspection.** The management should understand that the purpose of inspection is to improve the process and reduce its costs. Mass inspection occurs too late in the process, it is expensive and ineffective. Quality results from prevention of defectives through process improvement but not inspection.

(*d*) **Stop awarding business based on price alone.** Don't award the business to suppliers on the basis of price alone, but also consider also quality. The goal is to have a single supplier for each item to develop loyalty and trust and hence to provide improved products and services. Preference should be given to suppliers who use modern methods of quality improvement in their business.

(*e*) **Improve constantly and forever the system.** Management must take more responsibility to improve the quality and productivity, continually. The focus is on continuous improvement by preventing problems for reducing the cost of production. Minor variation is expected among products and services with the usage of statistical tools.

(*f*) **Institute training.** Management should practice the modern training methods and invest in training for all employees to perform their jobs in the best manner possible. Every employee should be trained in statistical methods that should be used to monitor the needs for further training.

(*g*) **Teach and institute leadership.** It is the management responsibility to teach and institute leadership quality for further supervision. The supervision should be focused to create a positive and supportive atmosphere to help the employees. The main goal of the supervision should be to improve the work system and product.

(*h*) **Drive out fear, create trust and create a climate for innovation.** Management should encourage open, team work and drive out fear regarding job security, physical dangers, performance appraisals, ignorance of organizational goals, poor supervision and unknown job. When people are working without fear trust is created and they will work for the general good of the organization. Hence, in this climate, people will create new ideas for improvement.

(*i*) **Optimize the efforts of teams, groups and staff areas.** Breakdown the barriers between the departments, among the levels of management, and between all the functional areas of the business. When the barriers are removed, the people can work as a team. Team work among different organizational units is essential for effective quality and productivity improvement.

(*j*) **Eliminate exhortations for the work force.** Eliminate slogans, exhortations, targets, numerical goals for the work force. A target such as **zero defects** is useless. Without a plan for the achievement of this objective. Hence goals should be set that are achievable by the workers. The tools and methods should be made available to improve the process.

(*k*) **Eliminate numerical quotas for the workforce.** Eliminate numerical quotas for the workforce and goals for management. When goals or targets are set, workers may shortcut quality to reach the goal. Quotas should be replaced with statistical methods of process control.

(*l*) **Remove barriers that rob people of pride of workmanship.** Remove the barriers that discourage employees from doing their jobs. Management must listen to employee suggestions, comments, and complaints, when workers are proud of their work, they will work to the fullest extend of their job. A barrier for people on salary is the annual rating (merit rating) of their performance.

(*m*) **Encourage education and self improvement for everyone.** Institute an ongoing program of training, education, and self improvement for all employees. A long term commitment to continuously train and educate people must be made by management. Everyone should be retrained as the organization requirements change to meet the changing environment.

(*n*) **Take action to accomplish the transformation.** Management has to accept the primary responsibility for the on-going improvement of the process. It has to create a corporate structure to implement the philosophy. A cultural change is required to previous **"business as usual attitude"** attitude. Management must be committed, involved and accessible if the organization is to succeed in implementing the new philosophy.

Unit 2 TQM PRINCIPLES

2.1 CUSTOMER SATISFACTION—CONCEPT

The most important asset of any organization is its customers. An organization's success depends on how many customers it has, how much they buy, and how often they buys. Customers that are satisfied will increase in number, buy more, and buy more frequently. Satisfied customers also pay their bills promptly, which greatly improves cash flow the lifeblood of any organization. Increasingly, manufacturing and service organizations are using customer satisfaction as the measure of quality. The importance of customer satisfaction is not only due to national competition but also due to worldwide competition. This is reflected in the Malcolm Baldrige National Quality Award, where customer satisfaction accounts for 30% of the total points.

Total Quality Management (TQM) implies an organizational productivity with meeting the customer expectations, so that customers are delighted. Understanding the customer's needs and expectations is essential to winning new business and keeping existing business. An organization must give its customers a quality product or service that meets their needs at a reasonable price, which includes on-time delivery and outstanding service.

2.2 WHO IS THE CUSTOMER?

According to Gandhiji, the customers are:

- *The most important people in the business.*
- *Not dependent on the organization. The organization depends on them.*
- *Not an interruption to work but are the purpose of it.*
- *Doing a favour when they seek business and not vice-versa.*

- *A part of business, not outsiders.*
- *Life blood of the business.*
- *People who come with their needs and jobs.*
- *Deserve the most courteous and attentive treatment.*

There are two distinct types of customers:

- External
- Internal.

An external customer is those use the product or service, or the one who purchases the product or service, or the one who influences the sale of the product or service. An external customer exists outside the organization and generally falls into three categories:

- Current,
- Prospective,
- Lost customers.

Each category provides valuable customer satisfaction information for the organization. Every employee in the organization must know how their job enhances the total satisfaction of the external customer.

An internal customer is just as important. Every function, whether it be engineering, order processing, or production, has an internal customer each receives a product or service and, in exchange, provides a product or service.

Every person in a process is considered a customer of the preceding operation. Each worker's goal is to make sure that the quality meets the expectations of the next person. When that happens throughout the manufacturing, sales, and distribution chain, the satisfaction of the external customer should be assured.

The basic concept of TQM is an unwavering focus on customers, both internal and external. Most employees know about the external customer. The formula for successful internal customer/ supplier relationships varies. But it always begins with people asking their internal customers three basic questions:

What do you need from me?

What do you do with my output?

Are there any gaps between what you need and what you get?

2.3 CUSTOMER SATISFACTION MODEL

Teboul's model of customer satisfaction represented by the circle, and the square represents the product or service offered by the company. The customer needs intersection portion, shown with dots, is perceived as the customer satisfaction. So it is understood that the company should strive for increasing the intersection customer satisfaction.

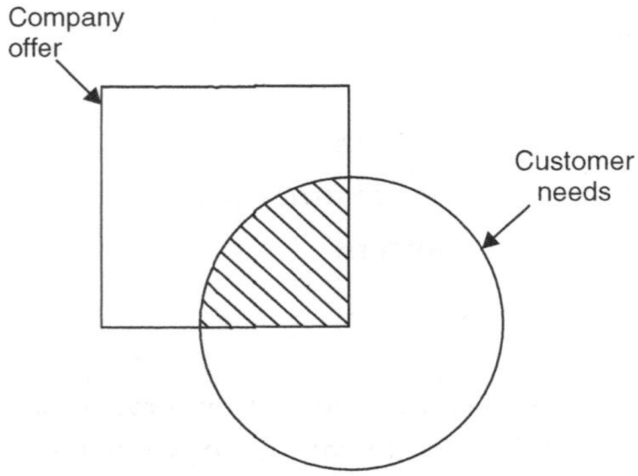

FIGURE 2.1 **Customer Satisfaction Model**

2.4 CUSTOMER-SUPPLIER CHAIN

In order to achieve the total customer orientation, TQM requires the better customer-supplier relationship. All processes require inputs, which are provided by the internal or external supplier. Similarly all processes deliver outputs, which are used by internal and external customers. Each unit is considered as a customer by the previous units and as a supplier for the next unit.

2.5 CUSTOMER PERCEPTION OF QUALITY

One of the basic concepts of the TQM philosophy is continuous process improvement. This concept implies that there is no acceptable quality level because the customer's needs, values, and expectations are constantly changing and becoming more demanding.

An American Society for Quality (ASQ) survey ranked the customer perceptions in the following order:

- Performance,
- Features,
- Service,
- Warranty,
- Price, and
- Reputation.

(*a*) **Performance.** Performance involves "fitness for use". It indicates that the product and service is ready for the customers' use at the time of sale. Other factors include

(*i*) Availability: It is the probability that a product will operate when needed,

(*ii*) Reliability: It is freedom from failure overtime, and

(*iii*) Maintainability: It is the ease of keeping the product operable.

(*b*) **Features.** Features are secondary characteristics of the product or service. For example, the primary function of a cell phone is for communication, whereas other facilities such as calculator and alarm are features of the cell phone.

(*c*) **Service.** Customer service is an intangible in nature. Intangible characteristics are those traits that are not quantifiable, but it contributes greatly to customer satisfaction.
The main organizations objective is to provide good quality of the product to the customer at the right time, even though the customers are not complaining about their service.

(*d*) **Warranty.** The product warranty represents an organization's public promise of a quality product. In other words, it represents a public commitment to guarantee a level of service sufficient to satisfy the customer. A warranty forces the organization to focus on the customer's definition of product and service quality. It also forces the organization to develop a corrective action system.

In present scenario, the warranty attracts and builds the market. It encourages customers to buy a service by reducing the risk of the purchase decision. Hence it generates more sales from existing customers by enhancing loyalty.

(*e*) **Price.** Nowadays customer is willing to pay a higher price to obtain value. Also customers expect high quality products at the lower price. Customers prefer the organizations that are providing the greatest value for their money. For this purpose, customers are constantly evaluating all the organizations. In our highly competitive environment, each customer's concept of value is continually changing. In order to overcome this challenge, the organizations should identify, verify and update each customer's perception of value in relation to each product and service regularly.

(*f*) **Reputation.** It is obvious that customers are willing to buy products or service from a known, trusted and reputed organization. The total customer satisfaction is based on, not only with the product, the entire experience with the organization. Thus reputation of a firm brings the market to them. So organization should strive for customers for life.

2.6 CUSTOMER COMPLAINTS (CUSTOMER FEEDBACK)

From many statistical analysis of customer satisfaction, the following conclusions were made.

(*i*) A totally satisfied customer contributes 2.6 times as much revenue to a company as a somewhat satisfied customer.

(*ii*) A totally satisfied customer contributes 17 times as much revenue as a somewhat dissatisfied customer.

(*iii*) A totally dissatisfied customer decreases revenue at a rate equal to 1.8 times of what a totally satisfied customer contributes to business.

Thus the number of dissatisfied customers should be reduced as much as possible. In order to do so, customer feedback must be continuously solicited and monitored.

2.6.1 Importance of Customer Feedback/Customer Complaint

Customer feedback or customer complaint is required

- to discover customer dissatisfaction,
- to identify customer's needs,
- to discover relative priorities of quality,
- to compare performance with the competition, and
- to determine opportunities, for improvement.

2.6.2 Tools Used for Collecting Customer Complaints

Following tools are used for collecting customer complaints:

(*a*) ***Comment card:*** It is a card, normally attached to the warranty card, issued with the product at the time of sales.

(*b*) ***Customer questionnaire***: It includes:

- Surveys through mail, or
- Surveys through E-mail, or
- Surveys through telephone.

(*c*) ***Focus groups***: It includes customer meetings, word associations, discussions, relaxation techniques, etc.

(*d*) ***Toll-free telephone numbers:*** Toll-free telephone numbers are an effective technique for receiving complaint feedback. Organizations can respond faster and more cheaply to the complaint, such a number does not, however, reach those who decided not to buy the product or those who discovered some likable feature on a competitor's product. Toll-free numbers are in use by at least 50% of all organizations with sales of at least ten billion dollars.

(*e*) ***Customer visits:*** Services should be held at least annually visits to a customer's place of business provide another way to gather information. An organization can proactively monitor its product's performance while it is in use and thereby identify any specific or recurring problems. Senior managers should be involved in these visits and not delegate them to someone else. However, it is a good idea to take along operating personnel so they can see first hand how the product is performing.

(*f*) ***Report card:*** Very effective information-gathering tool is the report card. The data are analysed to determine areas for improvement.

(*g*) ***The internet and computer:*** Some managers are beginning to monitor discussion that take place on the internet to find out what customers are saying about the product.

(*h*) ***Employee feedback:*** Employees are often an untapped source of information. Companies are listening more to the external customer but still are not listening to employees. Employees can offer insight into conditions that inhibit service quality in the organization. Employee groups can brainstorm ideas to come up with solution to the problems that customers have identified.

2.7 SERVICE QUALITY

Customer service is the set of activities an organization uses to satisfy the customers and their needs. The service can be provided at

(*a*) before the sale of the product ;

(*b*) during the sale of the product ; and

(*c*) after the sale of the product.

2.7.1 Elements of Customer Service

Jacques Horovitz and Chan Cudennec-poon have listed the 25 elements of customer service. They are:

(I) Organization

(*i*) Identify each market segment.

(*ii*) Write down the requirements.

(*iii*) Communicate the requirements.

(*iv*) Organize processes.

(*v*) Organize physical spaces.

(II) Customer Care

(*vi*) Meet the customer's expectations.

(*vii*) Get the customer's point of view.

(*viii*) Deliver what is promised.

(*ix*) Make the customer feel valued.

(*x*) Respond to all complaints.

(*xi*) Over-respond to the customer.

(*xii*) Provide a clean and comfortable customer reception area.

(III) Communication

(*xiii*) Optimize the trade-off between time and personal attention.

(*xiv*) Minimize the number of contact points.

(*xv*) Provide pleasant, knowledgeable and enthusiastic employees.

(*xvi*) Write documents in customer friendly language.

(IV) Front-line People

(*xvii*) Hire people who like people.

(*xviii*) Challenge them to develop better methods.

(*xix*) Given them the authority to solve problems.

(*xx*) Serve them as internal customers.

(*xxi*) Be sure they are adequately trained.

(*xxii*) Recognize and reward performance.

(V) Leadership

(*xxiii*) Lead by example.

(*xxiv*) Listen to the front-line people.

(*xxv*) Strive for continuous process improvement.

2.8 CUSTOMER RETENTION

Customer retention is the process of retaining the existing customers. It is obvious that customer retention is more powerful and effective than customer satisfaction. Customer care can be defined as every activity which occurs within an organization that ensures that a customer is not only satisfied but also retained.

The following research findings will enable us to understand the real significance customer retention. The important research findings are:

(*i*) Over 60% of an organization's future revenue will come from existing: customers.

(*ii*) A 2% increase in customer retention has an equivalent impact upon profitability as a 10% reduction in operating costs.

(*iii*) Upto 96% of unhappy customers do not infact complains. But they are three times more likely to communicate a bad experience to other customers than good one.

(*iv*) 91% of the unhappy customers will never purchase goods and services from you again.

(*v*) If you make an effort to remedy customers' complaints, 82 to 95% of them will stay on with you.

(*vi*) It costs 5 times as much to attract a new customer as it costs to keep an old one.

Thus the customer retention is more essential than attracting new customers.

Customer retention represents the activities that produce the necessary customer satisfaction that creates customer loyalty. Customer retention can be improved by obtaining customer feedback and by measuring customer satisfaction.

Customer feedback is obtained from customer satisfaction surveys, focus groups, interviews, and observations. Customer satisfaction should be measured by using the hard measures of cash register receipts, market share, the level of customer retention, and the number of referrals from customers.

Customer retention really moves the customer satisfaction to the next level called customer delight.

2.9 EMPLOYEE INVOLVEMENT

Employee involvement is the backbone of a TQM movement. An effective TQM effort requires the total involvement from every person at all levels in the organization. Employee involvement leads to meet the organization goals and objectives. It also improves the quality and productivity at all levels of the organization.

Some of the important aspects of employee involvement are:

- Employee motivation,
- Employee empowerment,
- Teams and teamwork,
- Recognition and reward schemes, and
- Performance appraisal.

2.9.1 Employee Motivation

(*a*) **Definition of Motivation.** Motivation is the process of inducing people inner drives and action towards certain goals and committing his energies to achieve these goals.

"Motivation means a process of stimulating people to accomplish desired goals."

—Scott

"Motivation is the process of attempting to influence others to do your will through the possibility of reward."

—Edwin B. Flippo

(*b*) **Importance of Motivation**

- Motivation improves employee involvement.
- Motivation promotes job satisfaction and thus reduces absenteeism and turnover.
- Motivation helps in securing a high level of performance and hence enhances efficiency and productivity.
- Motivation creates a congenial working atmosphere in the organization and thus promotes interpersonal cooperation.

(*c*) **Theories of Motivation.** There are many theories of motivation, the Maslow's hierarchy of needs theory and Hertzberg's two factor theories are more important in the concept of quality management.

Maslow's Need Hierarchy Theory

Maslow's theory is based on the human needs. Drawing chiefly on his clinical experience, he classified all human needs into a hierarchical manner from the lower to the higher order. In essence, he believed that once a given level of need is satisfied, it no longer serves to motivate man.

Moslow identified five levels in his need hierarchy as shown in the figure.

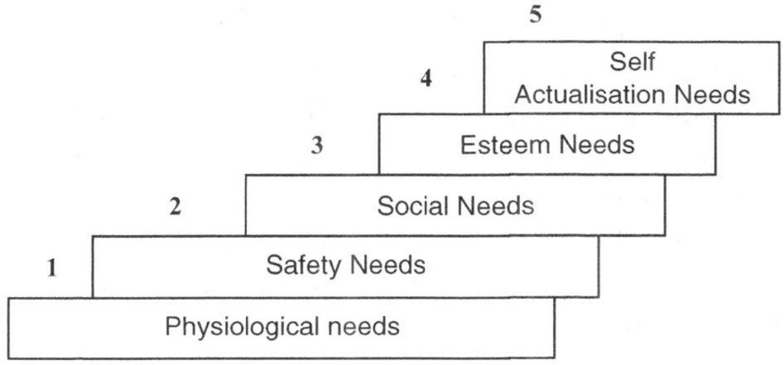

FIGURE 2.2 **Maslow's Need Hierarchy**

1. ***Physiological Needs.*** These needs are basic to human life and, hence, include food, clothing, shelter, air, water and other necessities of life. These needs are relate to the survival and maintenance of human life. They exert tremendous influence on human behaviour. These needs are to be met first at least partly before higher level needs emerge. Once physiological needs are satisfied, they no longer motivate the man.
2. ***Safety Needs.*** After satisfying the physiological needs, the next needs felt are called safety and security needs. These needs find expression such desires as economic security and protection from physical dangers. Meeting these needs requires more money and hence, the individual is prompted to work more. Like physiological needs, these become inactive once they are satisfied.
3. ***Social Needs.*** Man is a social being. He is therefore, interested in socal interaction, companionship, belongingness, etc. It is this socializing and belongingness why individuals prefer to work in groups and especially older people go to work.
4. ***Esteem Needs.*** These need refer to self-esteem and resolve respect. They include such needs, which indicate self-confidence, achievement, competence, knowledge and independence. The fulfillment of esteem needs leads to self-confidence, strength and capability of being useful in the organization. However, inability to fulfil these needs results in feelings like inferiority, weakness and helplessness.
5. ***Self-Actualization Needs.*** This level represents the culmination of all the lower, intermediate and higher needs of human beings. In other words, the final step under the need hierarchy model is the need for self-actualization. This refers to fulfillment.

According to Maslow, the human needs follow a definite sequence of domination. The second need does not arise until the first is reasonably satisfied, the third need does not emerge until the first two needs have been reasonably satisfied and so on.

Herzberg's Motivation Hygiene Theory

The psychologist Frederik Herzberg extended the work of Maslow and proposed a new motivation theory popularly known as Herzberg's Motivation Hygiene (Two-Factor) Theory. Herzberg conducted a widely reported motivation study of 200 accountants and engineers employed by firms in an around Western Pennsylvania. He asked these people to describe two important incidents at their jobs:

(*a*) When did you feel particularly good about your job? and

(*b*) When did you feel exceptionally bad about your job?

He asked the critical incident method of obtaining data. The responses when analyzed were found quite interesting and fairly consistent. The replies respondents gave when they felt good about their jobs were significantly different from the replies given when they felt bad. Reported good feelings were generally associated with job satisfaction whereas bad feelings with job dissatisfaction. Herzberg labeled the job satisfies motivators and he called job dissatisfies hygiene or maintenance factors. Taken together, the motivators and hygiene factors have become known as Herzberg's two-factor theory of motivation.

Herzberg's motivational and hygiene factors have shown in this table.

Hygiene: Job dissatisfaction	Motivators: Job satisfaction
	Achievement
	Recognition
	Work itself
	Responsibility
	Advancement
	Growth
Company Policy and	
Administration	
Supervision	
Interpersonal Relations	
Working Conditions	
Salary	
Status	
Security	

According to Herzberg, the opposite of satisfaction is not dissatisfaction. The underlying reason, he says, is that removal of dissatisfying characteristics from a job does not necessarily make the job satisfying. He believes in the existence of a dual continuum. The opposite of 'satisfaction' is no satisfaction and the opposite of 'dissatisfaction' is no 'dissatisfaction'.

According to Herzberg, today's motivators are tomorrow's hygiene because the latter stop influencing the behaviour of persons when they get them. Accordingly one's hygiene may be the motivator of another.

2.9.2 Employee Empowerment

(*a*) **Concept of Empowerment.** Empowerment is an environment in which people have the ability, the confidence, and the commitment to take the responsibility and ownership to improve the process and initiate the necessary steps to satisfy customer requirements within well-defined boundaries in order to achieve organisational values and goals.

Empowerment is the opposite of helplessness or dependency: An empowered person does not feel incapable of doing the things that he considers important for the well-being of his organisation. There are no constraints that he perceives to be externally imposed. In other words, being empowered implies that the person acts from a state of autonomy, doing what he knows is the right thing to do under a given set of circumstances.

It is understood that empowerment is dependent upon two factors

(*i*) An individual's personal choices; and

(*ii*) The organizational climate.

That can either encourage dependency or foster autonomy.

(*b*) **Definition of Empowerment.** *"The verb empower means `to give the means, ability or authority'. Therefore empowerment in work setting involves giving people the means, ability and authority to do something they have not done before."*

—Webster's dictionary

(*c*) **Job Enrichment Vs Job Empowerment.** Job enrichment is aimed at expanding the content of an individual's job. But job empowerment focuses on expanding on the context of the job such as its interactions and interdependencies to other functions of the organization.

(*d*) **Principles for Empowering Employees.** The following general principles may be used to empower the employees.

- Tell people what their responsibilities are.
- Give them authority equal to the responsibility assigned to them.
- Set standards of excellence.
- Provide them with training that will enable them to maintain standards.
- Give them knowledge and information.
- Provide them with feedback on their performance.
- Trust them and create trust worthiness in the organization.
- Allow them to fail but guide them and counsel them when needed.
- Treat them with dignity and respect.

(*e*) **Conditions to Create the Empowered Environment.** The three conditions required to create the empowered environment are:

- Everyone must understand the need for change.
- The system needs to change to the new paradigm.
- The organisation must provide information, education, and skill to its employees.

(*f*) **Characteristics of Empowered Employees.** The important characteristics of empowered employees, identified by Hubert Rampersad, are that

(*a*) They feel responsible for their own task.

(*b*) They are given a free hand in their work.

(*c*) They balance their own goals with those of the organization.

(*d*) They are well trained, equipped, creative, and customer oriented.

(*e*) They are critical, have self-esteem, and are motivated.

(*f*) They are challenged and encouraged.

(*g*) They monitor and improve their work continuously.

(*h*) They find new goals and change challenges.

Therefore, it is important to empower individuals and teams at all levels of the organization to achieve the continuous improvement process.

2.9.3 Teams and Teamwork

(*a*) **Meaning of Team and Teamwork.** A team can be defined as a group of people working together to achieve common objectives or goals.

Teamwork is the cumulative actions of the team during which each member of team subordinates his individual interests and opinions to fulfill the objectives or goals of the group.

TQM is based on the involvement of everyone in making improvements. So working in teams is an inseparable part of the TQM environment. Nowadays teamwork is adopted universally as the organisational mechanism for involving people in quality improvements.

(*b*) **Types of Teams.** Teams can be classified into four major groups. They are:

- Process improvement team,
- Cross-functional team,
- Natural work team, and
- Self-directed/self-managed work team.

(*i*) ***Process Improvement Team.*** Process improvement team focuses its attention on improvements of a process which is already operating to a satisfactory level with agreed to tolerances. They are meant for each operation of the process or sub-process. The scope of the team is limited to work unit. Team comprise of six to ten members from the work unit.

Depending upon the location of the sub-process, the internal or external supplier as well as internal or external customer is also included in the team. The life cycle of the team is temporary, because whenever the objective is reached, the team is disbanded.

(*ii*) ***Cross-functional Team.*** At the top management level, the cross-functional teams are formed by certain organizations which are very successful in solving complex problems involving functions of various departments. Six to ten members are selected from various functional areas of management to constitute cross-functional teams.

Cross-functional teams may discuss the complex problems and break these down into parts and refer these to departmental teams and work teams of respective functions for further solution. Feedback in the form of solutions is gathered and the problem as a whole is solved at the level of cross-functional teams. This team is also temporary.

(*iii*) ***Natural Work Team.*** Team comprises of all the members of the work unit and the team members are not volunteer; they are selected by management. Manager is also a part of the team and he is selecting the projects to be improved. Some employees may not cooperating in team work for variety of reasons. So that the manager is in a position to motivate the employees in a proper direction and make them to feel comfortable in the team.

(*iv*) ***Self-directed (or) Self-managed Work Team.*** A self-managing team is a group of individuals which works together continuously. These teams plan, execute and control their work to achieve a defined output. The team consists of members from the work unit except supervisor. The team coordinator is selected within the team in consultation with the top management and that may rotate among members.

The team should meet daily to plan their activities and the decisions are usually made by consensus. Additional responsibilities of the teams are hiring/dismissal, performance evaluation, customer relations, supplier relations, recognition/reward and training.

(*c*) **Characteristics of Successful Teams.** The effective team should have certain characteristics. These are explained as follows:

(*i*) ***Sponsor:*** In order to have effective liaison with the quality council, there should be a sponsor. The sponsor is a person from the quality council; he is to provide support to the organization.

(*ii*) ***Team Charter:*** A team charter is a document that defines the team's mission, boundaries, the background of the problem, the team's authority and duties, and resources. It also identifies the members and their assigned roles are leader, recorder, time keeper and facilitator.

(*iii*) ***Team Composition:*** The size of the team should not exceed ten members except in the case of natural work teams or self-directed teams. Teams should be divorced by having members with different skills, perspectives and potential. Wherever needed, the internal and external customers and suppliers should be included as a team member.

(*iv*) ***Training:*** The team members should be trained in the problem-solving techniques, team dynamics and communication skills.

(*v*) ***Ground Rules:*** The team should have separate rules of operation and conduct. Ground rules should be discussed with the members, whenever needed it should be reviewed and revised.

(*vi*) ***Clear Objectives:*** The objective of the team should be stated clearly. Without the clear objective, the team functions are not to be effective.

(*vii*) ***Accountability:*** The team performance is accountable. Periodic status report of the team should be given to the quality council. The team should review its performance to determine possible team process weaknesses and make improvements.

(*viii*) ***Well-defined Decision Procedures:*** The decision should be made clearly at the right time by the team.

(*ix*) ***Resources:*** The adequate information should be given to the team wherever needed. The team cannot be expected to perform successfully without the necessary tools.

(*x*) ***Trust:*** Management must trust the team to perform the task effectively. There must also be trust among the members and a belief in each other.

(*xi*) ***Effective Problem-solving:*** Problem-solving methods are used to make the effective decision.

(*xii*) ***Open Communication:*** Open communication should be encouraged *i.e.*, everyone feels free to speak in the team whatever they are thinking, without any interruptions.

(*xiii*) ***Appropriate Leadership:*** Leadership is important in all the team. Leader is a person who leads the team, motivates the team and guides the team in a proper direction.

(*xiv*) ***Balanced Participation:*** Everyone in a team should be involved in the team's activities by voicing their opinions, lending their knowledge and encouraging other members to take part.

(*xv*) ***Cohesiveness:*** Members should be comfortable working with each other and act as a single unit, not as individuals or subgroups.

(*d*) **Elements of Effective Teamwork.** Following are the elements of effective teamwork:

- Purpose,
- Role and responsibilities,
- Activities,
- Effectiveness,
- Decisions,
- Results, and
- Recognition.

(*e*) **Reasons for Teams Work.** Teams work because many heads are more knowledgeable than one

- Each member of the team has special abilities that can be used to solve problems.
- Many processes are so complex that one person cannot be knowledgeable concerning the entire process and the whole is greater than the sum of its members.
- The interaction within the team produces results that exceed the contributions of each member.
- Third, team members develop a rapport with each other that allows them to do a better job.
- Finally, teams provide the vehicle for improved communication, thereby increasing the likelihood of a successful solution.

(*f*) **Activities of Team Management Wheel.** The team management wheel emphasizes the following activities:

- ***Advising:*** Giving and gaining information.
- ***Innovating:*** Creating and experimenting with ideas.
- ***Promoting:*** Exploring and presenting opportunities.
- ***Developing:*** Assessing and planning application.
- ***Organizing:*** Arranging for resources and implementation.
- ***Producing:*** Concluding and delivering outputs.
- ***Inspecting:*** Controlling and auditing procedures.
- ***Maintaining:*** Upholding and enforcing standards.
- ***Linking:*** Establishing linkages.

(*g*) **Role of Team Members.** For effective teamwork, team members are required to perform a number of roles and responsibilities. Thus all team members should.

- Devote themselves to the common team goals based on a common mission and vision.
- Feel themselves responsible and equal.
- Be interested and motivated.
- Accept, appreciate, and respect each others.
- Give high priority continuous improvement
- Participate actively with the activities of the team.
- Offer, views, opinions and ideas freely and voluntarily.
- Trust, support, understand and have genuine concern for other team members.
- Attend training seriously with a receptive attitude.
- Abide by the decisions taken by the team.
- Be responsible for their own contribution as well as for the results of the team
- Encourage feedback on own behaviour.
- Be aware of and recognize their responsibility for improvement. Make personal improvement a routine.

(*h*) **Stages of Team Development.** Each team takes sometime to start functioning effectively towards problem solving. Each team goes through six distinct stages in its development. These are forming, storming, norming, performing, maintenance, and evaluating.

(*i*) ***Forming stage:*** When a team is created, it consists of group of individuals and team work does not exist at this stage. Team's purpose, members' roles, acceptance of roles, authority and process of functioning are learnt in the formation process.

(*ii*) ***Storming stage:*** Initial agreements and role allocations are challenged and re-established at this stage of team development. At this stage, hostilities and personal needs often emerge which may be resolved.

(*iii*) ***Norming stage:*** During norming stage of team development, formal and informal relationships get established among team members. Openness and cooperation have been observed as signs of team's behaviour.

(*iv*) ***Performing stage:*** At this stage, the team starts operating in successful manner. Trust, openness, healthy conflict and decisiveness of a group's performance can be reached at this stage.

(*v*) ***Maintenance stage:*** Functioning of team does not deteriorate overtime. At this stage, the performance of teamwork at the earlier stage will be maintained for some period of time.

(*vi*) ***Evaluating stage:*** At this stage, team's performance is to be evaluated in view of the set targets. Both self-evaluation and management-based evaluation form this stage of team development.

(*i*) **Barriers to Team Progress.** The various roadblocks to team progress are:

- Insufficient training.

- Incompatible rewards and compensation.
- First-line supervisor resistance.
- Lack of planning.
- Lack of management support.
- Access to information systems.
- Lack of union support.
- Project scope too large.
- Project objectives are not significant.
- No clear measures of success.
- No time to do improvement work.

(*j*) **Benefits of Teamwork.** The benefits of teamwork include:

- Improved solutions to quality problems.
- Improved ownership of solutions.
- Improved communications.
- Improved integration.

2.9.4 Recognition and Reward

(*a*) **Meaning of Recognition.** Recognition is a process whereby management shows acknowledgement of an employee's outstanding performance. Recognition is a form of employee positive motivation. Recognition of employees is highly essential as people find themselves in an accepted and winning role. To sustain employee's interest and to propel them towards improvement, it is essential to recognize the people. This acknowledgement may be of financial, psychological or both in nature.

(*b*) **Reasons for Recognizing the Employees.** The employee's effort towards the improvement should be recognized for many reasons. Recognition is essential to:

— Improve employee's morale.

— Show the company's appreciation for better performance.

— Create satisfied workplace.

— Create highly motivated workplace.

— Reinforce behavioural patterns.

— Stimulate creative efforts.

(*c*) **Meaning of Reward.** Reward is a tangible one, such as increased salaries, commissions, cash bonus, gain sharing, etc., to promote desirable behaviour.

(*d*) **Types of Rewards.** Broadly, one can classify the rewarding systems into two groups. They are:

- ***Intrinsic rewards:*** These are related to feelings of accomplishment or self-worth.
- ***Extrinsic rewards:*** These are related to pay or compensation issues.

Intrinsic Vs Extrinsic rewards

Intrinsic Rewards	Extrinsic Rewards
1. Non-monetary forms of recognition to acknowledge achievement of quality improvement goals.	1. Profit sharing
2. Celebrations to acknowledge achievement of quality improvement goals.	2. Gain sharing
3. Regular expressions of appreciation by managers and leaders to employees to acknowledge achievement of quality improvement goals.	3. Employment security
4. 360° performance appraisals - feedback from co-workers (other than the immediate supervisor), subordinates or customers is incorporated into performance appraisals.	4. Compensation time
5. Formal suggestion system available for individuals to make quality improvement suggestions.	5. Individual based performance systems
6. Developmental based performance appraisals.	6. Quality based performance appraisals
7. Quality based promotions.	7. Customer Satisfaction and Employee Involvement

Source: Richard S. Allen and Ralph H. Kilmann

2.9.5 Performance Appraisal

(*a*) **Meaning of Performance Appraisal.** Performance appraisal is a systematic and objective assessment or evaluation of performance and contribution of an individual. It is a systematic and objective way of judging the relative worth of an employee in performing his/her task. It is the systematic, periodic and an impartial rating of an employee's excellence in matters pertaining to his present job and his potential for a better job.

(*b*) **Need for Performance Appraisal.** The purpose of performance appraisal is:

- To identify employees for salary revision, promotion, transfer, demotion, and lay-off.
- To take an organisational of inventory people, skills and potential for comparing it with its needs.
- To determine training and development needs of the employees.
- To motivate employees by providing feedback on their performance levels.
- To know personal strengths and weaknesses of different individuals.
- To establish a basis for research and reference for personnel decisions in future.
- To guide the individual to plan job and personal objectives and to help him in career planning.
- To validate the selection procedures.

- To improve communication in an organization.
- To make the supervisors and executives more observant of their subordinates.

(*c*) **Process of Performance Appraisal (Steps in Development of Appraisal System).** There are six steps in the development of appraisal system. The following chart depicts the self-explanatory steps required for the process of performance appraisal.

1. Establish performance standards
↓
2. Communicate performance expectations to employees
↓
3. Measure actual performance
↓
4. Compare actual performance with standards
↓
5. Discuss the appraisal with the employee
↓
6. If necessary, initiate correction action

(*d*) **Benefits of Performance Appraisal.** The performance appraisal benefits include:

- It provides useful feedback to the employee, supervisor and personnel specialists and allows them to take corrective measures to improve performance further.
- It helps in determining the pay adjustments, increments and bonuses as it rates the merit of the employee.
- It provides basis for employee promotion, transfer of demotion.
- It helps in determining individual's training and developmental needs and in designing training programmes accordingly.
- It helps the employee to plan their career.
- It helps in evaluating the staffing or personnel department procedures and provides feedback on their strengths and weaknesses.
- It may provide information on some external factors such as family circumstances, health, financial or personal matters that may be affecting the performance.
- It puts a sort of pressure on people for better performance. It makes him realise that he is being continuously observed and his improvements are being noted.

(*e*) **Performance Measures.** Performance measures indicate the measurement of success in an organization.

(*f*) **Objectives of Performance Measures.** Ray F. Boedecker has identified and listed seven objectives of performance measures. The seven objectives are:

- To establish baseline measures and reveal trends.
- To determine which processes need to be improved.

- To indicate process gains and losses.
- To compare goals with actual performance.
- To provide information for individual and team evaluation.
- To provide information to make informed decisions.
- To determine the overall performance of the organization.

(*g*) **Requirements (or Criteria) of the Performance Measures.** Successful implementation, the selected measures should try to satisfy the following requirements:

- Performance measures should be simple and understandable to the users.
- Instead of using many performance measures, it is preferable to use few numbers of key measures.
- While selecting measures, one should select the measures which are more relevant to customers.
- Performance measures should focus on continuous improvement, prevention and corrective action.
- Cost related performance measures should be preferred to better understand the financial position of the firm.
- The performance measures selected/used should be transparent and visible to all the employees.
- The performance measures should be time-based; preferably measures should be based on hourly, daily, or weekly rather than monthly or quarterly.
- The results of the, performance measures should balanced the interests of all stakeholders.

(*h*) **Strategy for Implementing Performance Measures.** The quality council has the overall responsibility for the performance measures. It ensures that all the measures are integrated into a total system of measures. To develop the system, the quality council will obtain appropriate information from all of the stake-holders. They utilize the core values, goals, mission, and vision statements as well as the objectives and the criteria given above. With this information, the strategic measurement system is created.

A typical example of a strategic measurement system of an organization is given below.

Criteria	Measurement system / measures / indicators
Quality	— % increase in quality grade — % reduction in failure rate — % reduction in cost of poor quality — reduction in number of customer's complaints — % reduction of rejects and scrap — % reduction of safety and environmental incidents

Throughput time	— reduction in throughput time — increase in manufacturing cycle effectiveness — reduction in number of breakdowns — increase in availability — increase in invoicing speed — reduction in time between order and delivery
Productivity	— increase in productivity — increase in effectiveness — increase in efficiency — increase in revenue growth — increase in sales and market growth — % reduction in personnel turnover
Added value	— increase in revenue per employee — increase in gross and net added value

(*i*) **Performance Measures Presentation.** The commonly used techniques for presenting performance measures are:

- Time series trend graphs,
- Control charts,
- Capability index,
- Taguchi's loss function,
- Cost of poor quality, and
- Quality awards.

2.10 CONTINUOUS PROCESS IMPROVEMENT

Introduction

Quality-based organizations should strive to achieve perfection by continuously improving the business and production processes. Perfection is impossible because the race is never over; however, we must continually strive for its attainment.

Improvement is made by

- Viewing all work as a process, whether it is associated with production or business activities.
- Making all processes effective, efficient, and adaptable.
- Anticipating changing customer needs.
- Controlling in-process performance using measures such as scrap reduction, cycle time, control charts, and so forth.
- Maintaining constructive dissatisfaction with the present level of performance.
- Eliminating waste and rework wherever it occurs.

- Investigating activities that do not add value to the product or service, with the aim of eliminating those activities.
- Eliminating nonconformities in all phases of everyone's work, even if the increment of improvement is small.
- Using benchmarking to improve competitive advantage.
- Innovating to achieve breakthroughs.
- Incorporating lessons learned into future activities.
- Using technical tools such as statistical process control (SPC), experimental design, benchmarking, quality function deployment (QFD), and so forth.

Process

Process refers to business and production activities of an organization. Business processes such as purchasing, engineering, accounting, and marketing are areas where nonconformance can represent an opportunity for substantial improvement.

Inputs may be materials, money, information, data, etc. Outputs may be information, data, products, service, etc. The output of one process also can be the input to another process.

Outputs usually require performance measures. They are designed to achieve certain desirable outcomes such as customer satisfaction. Feedback is provided in order to improve the process.

The process is the interaction of some combination of people, materials, equipment, method, measurement, and the environment to produce an outcome such as a product, a service, or an input to another process. In addition to having measurable input and output, a process must have value-added activities and repeatability. It must be effective, efficient, under control, and adaptable. In addition, it must adhere to certain conditions imposed by policies and constraints or regulations.

There are five basic ways to improve the process:

- Reduce resources,
- Reduce errors,
- Meet or exceed expectations of downstream customers,
- Make the process safer, and
- Make the process more satisfying to the person doing it.

First, a process that uses more resources than necessary is wasteful. Reports that are distributed to more people than necessary waste copying and distribution time, material, user read time and eventually files space.

Second, for the most part, errors are a sign of poor workmanship and require rework. Typing errors that are detected after the computer print out required opening the file, making the correction and printing the revised documents.

Third, by meeting or exceeding expectations of downstream customers, the process is improved. For example, the better the weld, the less grinding required, making the appearance of finish paint more pleasing.

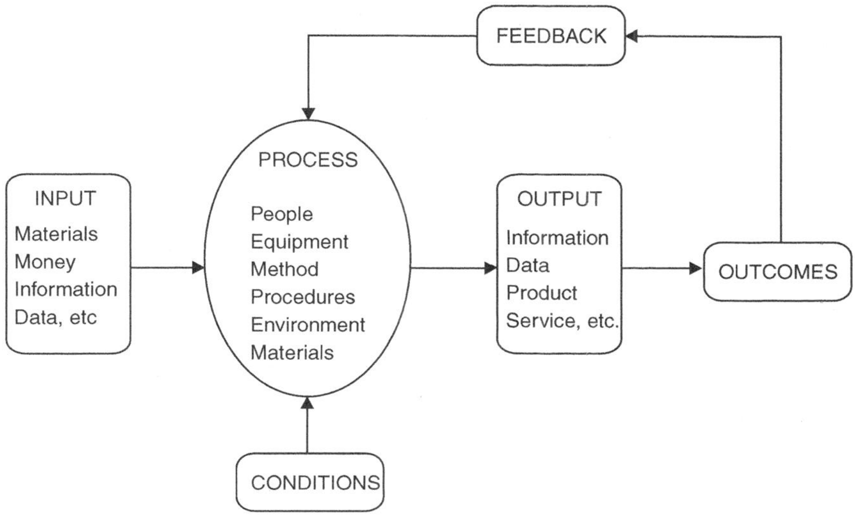

FIGURE 2.3 **Input/Output Process Model**

The fourth way a process can be improved is by making it safer. A safer workplace is more productive one with fewer lost-time accidents and less workers compensation claim.

The fifth way to improve a process is to increase the satisfaction of the individual performing the process. Sometimes a little change, such as an ergonomically correct chair, can make a substantial change in a person's attitude toward their work.

Continuous Process Improvement Approaches

The following continuous process improvement approaches have been successfully used by TQM practitioners.

- Juran Trilogy
- PDSA cycle
- 5S
- Kaizen

2.10.1 Juran Trilogy

Dr. Joseph M. Juran has contributed a lot to the movement of total quality. He is well known for his monumental, nearly 1900 page, text book on "Quality Control Handbook" and other contributions to the total quality. He highlighted managerial responsibility for quality and emphasized that quality can be achieved through people rather than techniques. He stressed both the management and technical aspects of quality management.

Juran divides quality management into three parts. They are:

- Quality planning,
- Quality control, and
- Quality improvement.

According to Juran, the planning process is crucial for improvement to become a continuous activity. Therefore, planning has to be conducted with a long-term view rather than a project by project basis.

(*a*) ***Quality Planning:*** For quality planning, Juran proposed, a self-explanatory planning road map, as shown in figure. During this planning stage, an organization prepares to meet established quality goals.

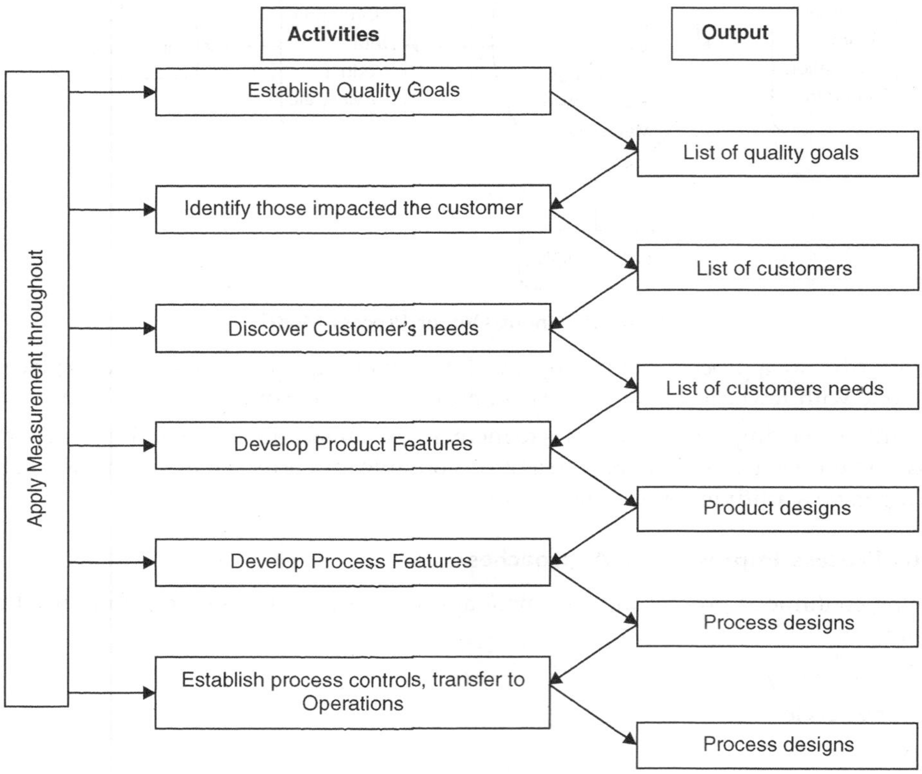

FIGURE 2.4 **Quality Planning Road Map (From Juran, 1990)**

(*b*) ***Quality Control:*** At this stage, control processes are designed to meet and ensure the quality goals set in the planning stage. With the help of the figure we can understand Juran's quality control process.

(*c*) ***Quality Improvement:*** The third part of the trilogy provides managers the means to find and remedy the basic causes of poor quality. It aims to attain levels of performance that are significantly higher than current levels. Juran's ten steps to quality improvement are presented in Table.

Juran's Ten Steps to Quality Improvement

1. Build awareness of the need and opportunity for improvement.
2. Set goals for improvement.
3. Organize to reach the goals.
4. Provide training.
5. Carry out projects to solve problems.
6. Report progress.
7. Give recognition.
8. Communicate results.
9. Keep score.
10. Maintain momentum by making annual improvement part of the regular systems and processes of the company.

Juran Trilogy Diagram

The figure shows the Juran trilogy diagram which is given below. It describes the way in which Juran's trilogy is designed to reduce the cost of quality over time.

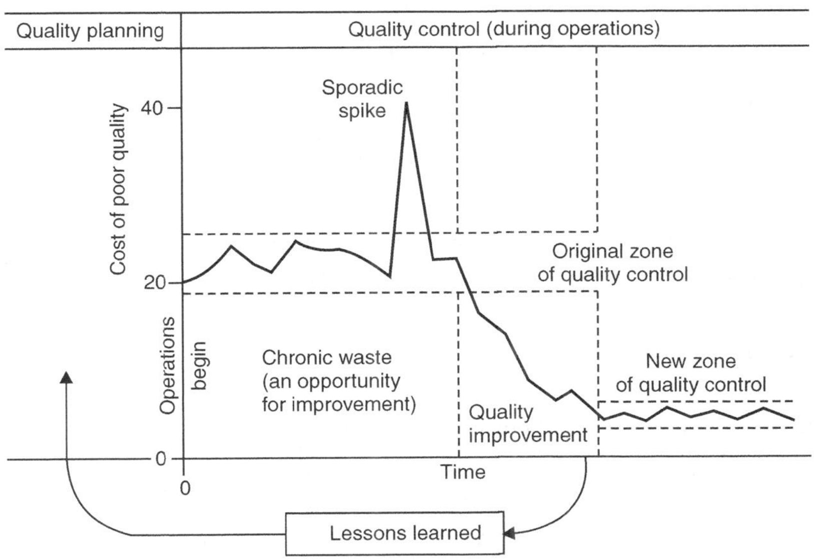

FIGURE 2.5 **Juran Trilogy Diagram**

In the above figure, Juran has made clear distinction between sporadic waste and chronic waste. The sporadic waste can be identified and corrected through quality control; whereas the chronic waste requires an improvement process. It is also clear that Juran's trilogy is a cyclic and ever-ending continuous process improvement approach.

2.10.2 PDSA Cycle (Or Deming Wheel)

The basic Plan-Do-Study-Act (PDSA) cycle was first developed by Shewhart and then modified by Deming. It is a model for testing ideas that you think may create plan improvement. It is an extremely practical common sense based approach that is easy to understand.

The four steps in the cycle are exactly as stated:

- First, plan carefully what is to be done.
- Second, carry out the plan (does it).
- Third, study the results. Did the plan work as intended, or were the results different?
- Finally, act on the results by identifying what worked as planned and what didn't?

Using the knowledge learned, develop an improved plan and repeat the cycle.

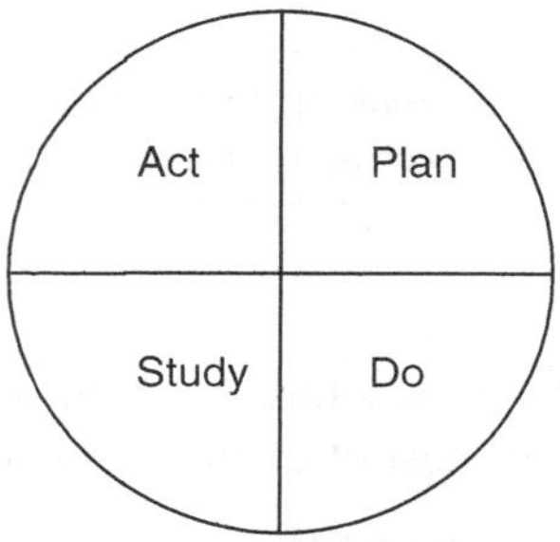

FIGURE 2.6 **PDSA Cycle**

(*a*) ***Phases of PDSA Cycle***

Phases	Description
Plan	Define the problem. Analyze the causes and draft an action plan for solving the problem. Determine the quality objectives and the critical factors. Define the performance indicators. Collect and analyze the necessary process data. Generate possible solutions. Select the most feasible solution; and work it out.
Do	First, implement the plan on a limited scale or conduct an experiment to test the proposed improvement. Collection data is hereby essential. Train all involved employees in the use of quality improvement methods and techniques. Describe the process which is considered for improvement and form project teams to lead the process.
Study	Evaluate the trial project with the performance indicators. Verify whether the improvement has been successful or not.

Act	Act to implement proven improvements. The choices are : Introduce the plan, adjust or reject it. The improvements are documented in standard procedures so all employees are well-informed on how to handle in future. Usually, the cycle will be repeated under the different circumstances and conditions to test how consistent the results are.

(*b*) ***Benefits of the PDSA Cycle:*** The benefits of the PDSA cycle can be experienced in the following areas:

- Daily routine management—for the individual and/or the team.
- Problem-solving process.
- Project management.
- Continuous development.
- Vendor development.
- Human resources development.
- New product development.

2.10.3 5W2H Method

The 5W2H stands for what, why, where, when, who, how, and how much. It is also a continuous improvement tool. The details of the 5W2H method are illustrated in the table.

Type	5W2H	Description	Countermeasure
Subject matter	What?	What is being done? Can this task be eliminated?	Eliminate unnecessary tasks.
Purpose	Why?	Why is this task necessary? Clarify the purpose.	
Location	Where?	Where is it being done? Does it have to be done there?	
Sequence	When?	When is the best time to do it? Does it have to be done then?	Change the sequence or combination.
People	Who?	Who is doing it? Should someone else do it? Why am I doing it?	
Method	How?	How is it being done? Is this the best method?Is there some other way?	Simplify the task.
Cost	How much?	How much does it cost now? What will the cost be after Improvement?	Select an improvement method.

2.10.4. 5S

(*a*) **Meaning of 5S.** The 5S practice is a house keeping technique used to establish and maintain a productive and quality environment in an organization. 5S was invented in Japan. It stands for five Japanese words that start with the letter 'S': SEIRI, SEITON, SEISO, SEIKETSU, and SHITSUKE.

A well-organized work place results in a safer, more efficient and more productive operation. It boosts the morale of the workers, promoting a sense of pride in their work and ownership of their responsibilities.

Sl.No.	Japanese Team	English Equivalent	Meaning in Japanese Context
1	SEIRI	Tidiness	Throw away all rubbish and unrelated materials in the work place.
2	SEITON	Orderliness	Set everything in proper place quick retrieval and storage.
3	SEISO	Cleanliness	Clean the work place, everything without fail.
4	SEIKETSU	Standardization	Standardizing the way of maintaining cleanliness.
5	SHITSUKE	Discipline	Practice 'FIVE S' daily. Make it a v of life. This also means commitment.

(*b*) **Objective of '5S'**

- To create a neat and clean work place.
- To systemise day to day working.
- To improve work efficiency.
- To standardize work practices.
- To improve work discipline.
- To improve the quality of work and products.

(*c*) **Factors in Implementing 5S.** The following factors are required for any organization to implement 5S concept successfully.

(*i*) ***Participation by all:*** 5S programme should be understood and practiced by all employees. Linkage with productivity, quality, cost, delivery, safety, and customer satisfaction should be clear to everyone.

(*ii*) ***Top management commitment:*** The CEO along with senior management team needs personally committed practice and supervise the programme. Without their deep commitment, no 5S can be successful.

(*iii*) ***Should be self sustaining:*** Banners, slogan posters and new tutors should be fully utilized to draw attention of everyone in the company. Basic in-house training and introduction to model companies would provide them the necessary skills.

(*iv*) ***Review the programme:*** Every month, a group of people selected from different areas of responsibility should tour the plant; evaluate each zone according to certain criteria of house keeping principles.

(*d*) **Benefits in Implementing 5S.** The benefits in implementing SS are as follows:

- Work place becomes clean and better organized. It becomes proud place to work.
- Results in good company image and generates more business.
- Shop floor and office operations become easier and safer.
- People become disciplined.
- Contribute to productivity quality and employee morale.
- Better quality awareness.
- More usable floor space.
- Lesser time wasted in material handling.
- Lower cost of production.
- Better preventive maintenance.
- High employee involvement.
- Lesser accidents.
- More time for improvement activities.

2.10.5 Kaizen

(*a*) **Meaning of Kaizen.** Kaizen is a Japanese word which means continuous improvement or improvement over improvement. It is the process of continuous improvements in small increments that make the process more efficient, effective, controllable, and adequate.

(*b*) **Tools of Kaizen.** The following are the tools which are used by kaizen in industries to achieve gradual and continuous improvement.

(*a*) ***5S techniques:*** house keeping.

(*b*) ***Just-in-Time(JIT):*** it principles namely JIT inventory and JIT manufacturing.

(*c*) ***Poka-yoke:*** a Japanese term which means mistake proofing.

(*d*) ***Muda:*** a Japanese term which means waste.

(*e*) ***Time and Motion study***

(*f*) ***Principles of material handling.***

(*g*) ***Clear identification of every thing in the organization for effective communication.***

(*c*) **Various Aspects of Kaizen.** The various aspects of Kaizen philosophy are shown in Fig. 2.7.

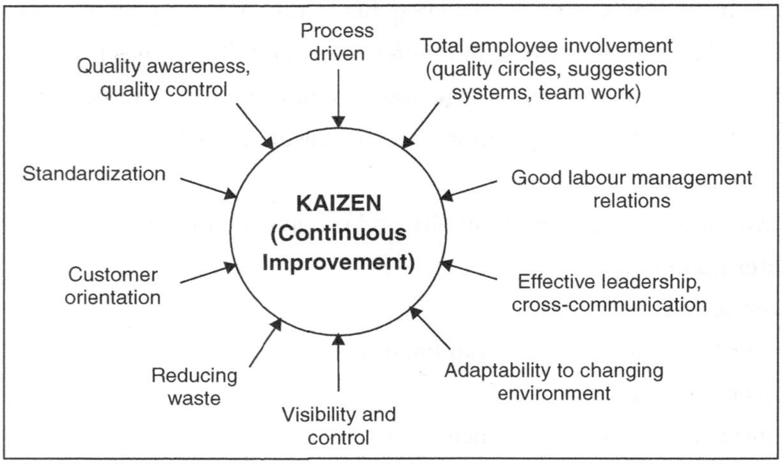

FIGURE 2.7 **Various Aspects of Kaizen Philosophy**

(*d*) **Features of Kaizen.** According to Glenn Gee et al, the Kaizen improvement focuses on the use of:

- Value-added and non-value-added work activities.
- Muda, which refers to the seven classes of wastes. Wastes are over-production, delay, transportation, processing, inventory, wasted motion, and defective parts.
- Principles of motion study and the use of cell technology.
- Principles of materials handling and use of one-piece flow.
- Documentation of standard operating procedures.
- The 5S for workplace organisation, which are five Japanese words that mean Proper arrangement (SEIRI), Orderliness (SEITON), Personal cleanliness (SEISO), Standardisation (SEIKETSU) and Discipline (SHITSUKE).
- Visual management by means of visual displays that everyone in the plant can use for better communication.
- Just-in-time principles to produce only the units in the right quantities, at the right time, and with the right resources.
- Poka-Yoke to prevent or detect errors.
- Team dynamics, which include problem solving, communication skills and conflict resolution.

(*e*) **Role of People in Implementing Kaizen**

- Top management must be committed to introducing Kaizen as a company strategy.
- The executives just below top management must formulate and carry out Kaizen goals according to guidelines from top management.
- Supervisors, like everyone else, must use Kaizen in their activities.
- Workers must be involved in Kaizen through the suggestions systems and small group activities.

(*f*) **Kaizen Vs Kairyo.** Both Kaizen and Kairyo are famous quality improvement approaches. In Kaizen (Japanese philosophy), improvements are accomplished gradually, *i.e.*, improvements in small increments. But Kairyo (Western philosophy) describes improvement through innovation, *i.e.*, improvements in one or two great jumps. Kairyo does not allow constant improvement.

It can be seen that Kaizen proceeds slowly, through gradual yet constant changes, whereas Kairyo proceeds in spurts, through major but irregular changes.

The main differences between Kaizen and Kairyo are listed below.

Kaizen (Continuous Improvement)	Kairyo (Innovation)
It is achieved through conventional know-how and PDCA.	It is obtained by technological or organizational breakthrough.
It is employee oriented.	It is technology oriented.
It requires little investment but great effort to maintain.	It requires large investment but little effort to maintain.
It involves everybody in the company.	It involves a selected few experts and researchers.
It requires recognition of effort before results.	It is motivated by expected results.

2.11 SUPPLIER PARTNERSHIP

2.11.1. Partnering—Meaning

Partnering is defined as a continuing relationship, between a buying firm and supplying firm, involving a commitment over an extended time period, an exchange of information, an acknowledgement of the risks and rewards of the relationship. The relationship between customer and supplier should be based upon trust, dedication to common goals and objectives, and an understanding of each party's expectations and values.

Japanese View on Partnering

The Japanese partnering concept is Keirestu. The key point of Keirestu is developing long term relationships with a few key suppliers rather than having short term relationship with many suppliers. Based upon a relationship of trust and long-term mutual interests, nowadays, many customer firms are willing to invest in a few key suppliers rather than requiring several suppliers constantly bid against each other.

Key Elements to Partnering

The three important elements to achieve the customer/supplier partnering relationship are

(*a*) ***Long-term commitment:*** Long-term commitment provides both customer and supplier the much needed environment to achieve the planned objectives. Because to set up and solve the problem of continuous improvement, both parties may require the sufficient time.

(*b*) ***Trust:*** Mutual trust between two parties forms the basis for a strong working relationship. Trust enables the partners to effectively combine their resources and knowledge. It results in a "win-win" situation for both partners.

(*c*) ***Shared vision:*** Both the customers and suppliers have the common goal, *i.e.*, to satisfy the end user. In order to ensure this goal, both parties should share and understand their goals and objectives. This concept is also known as mutual strategic planning.

Benefits of Partnering

The benefits of partnering include:

(*i*) Improved quality;
(*ii*) Reduced cost;
(*iii*) Increased productivity;
(*iv*) Increased efficiency;
(*v*) Increased market share;
(*vi*) Increased opportunity for innovation; and
(*vii*) Continuous improvement of products/services.

2.11.2 Supplier Sourcing

Three types of supplier sourcing are:

- Sole sourcing;
- Multiple sourcing, and
- Single sourcing.

(*a*) **Sole sourcing.** Sole sourcing is the use of only one supplier for the organization. The organization does not have any choice. It is forced to use only one supplier. This forced situation is because of the following factors: patents, technical specifications, raw material location, only one organization producing the item, etc.

(*b*) **Multiple sourcing.** Multiple sourcing is the use of two or more suppliers for an item. The basic concept of multiple sourcing is that competition will result in better quality, lower costs, and better service. The selection of suppliers from various alternatives is based on their performance in terms of price, quality and delivery.

(*c*) **Single sourcing.** Single sourcing is the use of one supplier for an item when several sources are available. It leads to long-term partnering relationship.

2.11.3 Supplier Selection

Usually suppliers are selected based on their performance in terms of cost, quality, delivery and reliability. In addition, supplier criteria include factors such as management compatibility, goal congruence, and strategic direction of the supplier firm.

Stages in Supplier Selection and Evaluation

There are four stages in supplier selection and evaluation. They are:

(*a*) ***Survey Stage:*** In survey stage, based on the information available through catalogues, advertisements, brochures, etc., a list is drawn up for further investigation.

(*b*) ***Enquiry Stage:*** In enquiry stage, a detailed analysis is made after obtaining required information. Standard enquiry forms are sent to the vendors, requesting them to furnish information. This may be followed by plant visit if necessary to have first hand details. The vendor's present customers may be enquired regarding his performance, promptness delivery, etc.

(*c*) ***Negotiation and Selection Stage:*** During the enquiry stage itself, many of the vendors might have been dropped from the original list as unsatisfactory. The remaining vendors may be called for direct negotiations to discuss various terms and conditions like payment terms, discounts, supply procedures, quality control procedures, etc... As a result of this a final list approved vendors is drawn up.

(*d*) ***Experience Stage:*** In this stage, the performance of the supplier is evaluated main basis of quality and promptness in delivery. A history card is maintained for each vendor. The card contains information like dates of supply of materials of by vendor, inspection procedure adopted, and acceptance or otherwise of the lost supplied. Frequent rejections may upset the production schedule in the buyer's company and result in heavy losses, hence such vendors might be dropped from the list. Similarly the late deliveries may cause stoppages in production; otherwise large inventories may have to be carried in stock. Both the situations are not desirable and hence such vendors are also reviewed for continuance as suppliers.

Conditions for Selection and Evaluation of Suppliers

Dr. Kaoru Ishikawa has suggested ten conditions for selection and evaluation of suppliers. His ten conditions are listed below.

Sl.No.	Suggestions
1	The supplier should understand and appreciate the management philosophy of the organization.
2	The supplier should have a stable management system.
3	The supplier should maintain high technical standards and have the capability of dealing with future technological innovations.
4	The supplier should provide those raw materials and parts required by the purchaser and those supplied meet the quality specifications.
5	The supplier should have the capability to produce the amount of production needed.
6	The supplier should not breach the corporate secrets.
7	The supplier should be easily accessible in terms of transportation and communication.
8	The supplier should be sincere in implementing the contract provisions.
9	The supplier should have an effective quality system and improvement program such as ISO/QS 9000.
10	The supplier should have a track record of customer satisfaction and organization credibility.

2.11.4 Supplier Rating

Meaning of Supplier Rating

A supplier rating system, also referred as a score card system, is used to obtain an overall rating of supplier performance. It is analogous to student's progress report. Usually supplier rating is based on quality, price, and performance and production capability.

Objectives of Supplier Rating

The customer rates supplier in order to:

- — obtain an overall rating of supplier performance;
- — ensure complete communication with suppliers;
- — provide each supplier about the details of problems for corrective action; and
- — maintain and improve the partnering relationship between the customer and the supplier.

Supplier Rating Format

The following table shows a model supplier rating format, otherwise known as supplier scorecard.

Rating scale:

5.0 - Very Good, 4.0 - Good, 3.0 - Average, 2.0 - Poor, 1.0 - Very Poor, 0 - Negative.

Item :	Rated by :			Date :		
Period : Location :		Supplier A	Supplier B	Supplier C	Supplier D	Supplier E
Quality Performance	Maximum Points	Actual Points	Actual Points	Actual Points	Actual Points	Actual Points
I. QUALITY (*i*) Quality personnel						
(*ii*) Quality procedure						
(*iii*) Concern for quality						
(*iv*) Concern history						
II. PRICE (*i*) Price-quality						
(*ii*) Price-negotiation						
(*iii*) Financial ability						
III. PERFORMANCE (*i*) Technical						
(*ii*) Delivery history						
(*iii*) Technical assistance						
IV. PRODUCTION CAPABILITY (*i*) Production capacity						
(*ii*) Manufacturing equipment						

2.11.5 Relationship Development

Relationship Development refers to maintaining and improving the growth of the customer-supplier relationship.

The partnering relationship between the customer and the supplier can be developed through:

(*a*) **Inspection.** The four phases of quality inspection are: (*i*) 100% inspection, (*ii*) sampling inspection, (*iii*) inspection audit, and (*iv*) identify check.

(*i*) In 100% inspection phase, all the items supplied by the suppliers are inspected. If the customer is satisfied with supplier in this phase for a period of time, then he gains confidence that initiates him to do sampling inspection rather than 100% inspection.

(*ii*) If the customer gains in this sampling inspection, then the customer changes to auditing the supplier's performance.

(*iii*) At this audit phase, the customer has complete confidence in the supplier and initiates identity checks.

(*iv*) The fourth and final phase occurs when both the customer and supplier perform only identity checks.

(*b*) **Training.** Both customers and suppliers should be trained in quality, team work, and other management aspects. Usually customers invite the suppliers to attend their seminars, workshops, courses, exhibition, etc. The training methods could improve the two parties relationship.

(*c*) **Team Approach.** Customer-supplier teams should be established in all the functional areas. Suppliers should be called for the team meetings of customers. Team meetings should occur at both partner's workplace. It may help in understanding each other's processes.

(*d*) **Recognition.** The customers can recognize the suppliers by awarding them non-monetary and/or monetary rewards. This reward and recognition concept will certainly improve the customer-supplier relationship.

Unit 3

STATISTICAL PROCESS CONTROL (SPC)

3.1 INTRODUCTION

It is practically not feasible to produce any two identical or similar products in the first time. If the product is to be designed or fabricated as per the prescribed norms of customers, it is usually produced by a repeatable or stable process. The quality of any product is determined by a specific process to the employed. The desired process must have the minimal variations with regard to the characteristics of the quality of the product. The problem solving tool by which the quantitative techniques are applied to achieve the process stability and to improve the capability by reducing the variability is known as Statistical Process Control (SPC).

3.2 OBJECTIVES OF SPC

- To control the quality of the processes and to ensure the end products as planned.
- To produce products and services with quality consistently.
- To improve the performance of processes continuously in order to meet the customer requirement.
- To find out the variations for improving the quality.
- To identify improvement opportunities and to assist in reducing variability by eliminating waste.

3.3 THE SEVEN SPC TOOLS OF QUALITY

The seven major SPC problem solving tools proposed by Prof. Ishikawa are:

- Process flow-diagrams
- Cause and effect diagram
- Histogram
- Pareto diagram
- Check sheet
- Scatter diagram and
- Control charts

3.3.1 Process Flow Diagram

A chart that represents a process is called as a process chart. It shows the overall picture of the sequence of operations connected with the manufacturing process graphically or diagrammatically. Each process involves men, machines, materials, methods and specifications, that are all used for providing a service or manufacturing a product. The following symbols are used to draw the process flow diagrams.

Sl.No.	Symbols	Shape	Description
1.	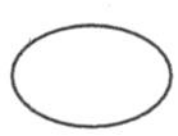	Ellipse	Start/End of process.
2.	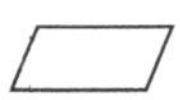	Parallelogram	Input/output in formations.
3.	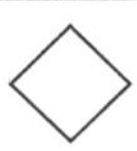	Diamond	Inspection/Decision-making (check the dimension and quality of the product).
4.	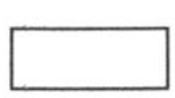	Rectangle	Operations/tasks/activities involved in a process.
5.	———	Line	Used to connect the chart.
6.	———→	Line with arrow	Used to show the direction of flow.
7.	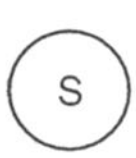	Circle with a letter inside	Used to continue the chart at another place with the same symbol.

3.3.2 Cause Effect Diagram

The cause and effect (C&E) diagram is a picture composed of lines and symbols designed to represent a meaningful relationship between an effect and its causes. It was developed by Dr. Kaoru Ishikawa in 1943 and is sometimes referred to as an Ishikawa diagram. This diagram, also called the Ishikawa or fishbone diagram, is used to associate multiple possible causes with a single effect. Thus, given a particular effect, the diagram is constructed to identify and organize the possible causes for it.

The primary branch represents the effect (the quality characteristics that is intended to be improved and controlled) and is typically labeled on the right side of the diagram. Each major branch of the diagram corresponds to a major cause (or class of causes) that directly relates to the effect. Minor branches correspond to more detailed causal factors. This type of diagram is useful in any analysis as it illustrates the relationship between cause and effect in a rational manner.

The cause and effect diagram is the brainchild of Kaoru Ishikawa, who pioneered quality management processes in the Kawasaki shipyards. In the process, he became one of the founding fathers of modern management. The cause and effect diagram is used to explore the potential or real causes (or inputs) that result in a single effect (or output). Causes are arranged according to their level of importance or detail, resulting in a depiction of relationships and hierarchy of events. This can help you search for the root causes, identify areas where there may be problems and compare the relative importance of different causes.

Causes in a cause and effect diagram are frequently arranged in four major categories. While these categories can be anything such as Manpower, methods, materials and machinery (recommended for manufacturing) and Equipment, policies, procedures and people (recommended for administration and service). These guidelines can be helpful but should not be used if they limit the diagram or are inappropriate.

Steps in Constructing a Cause and Effect Diagram

- Write the issue (problem or process condition) on the right side of the Cause and Effect diagram.
- Identify the major cause categories and write them in the four boxes on the Cause and Effect diagram. You may summarize the causes under categories such as manufacturing (Methods, machines, materials, manpower) and services (Places, procedures, people, policies) and environment (Surroundings, suppliers, system, skills).
- Brainstorm the potential causes of the problem. As the possible causes are provided, decide as group where to place them on the Cause and Effect diagram. It is acceptable to list a possible cause under more than one major cause category.
- Review each major cause category. Circle the most likely causes on the diagram.

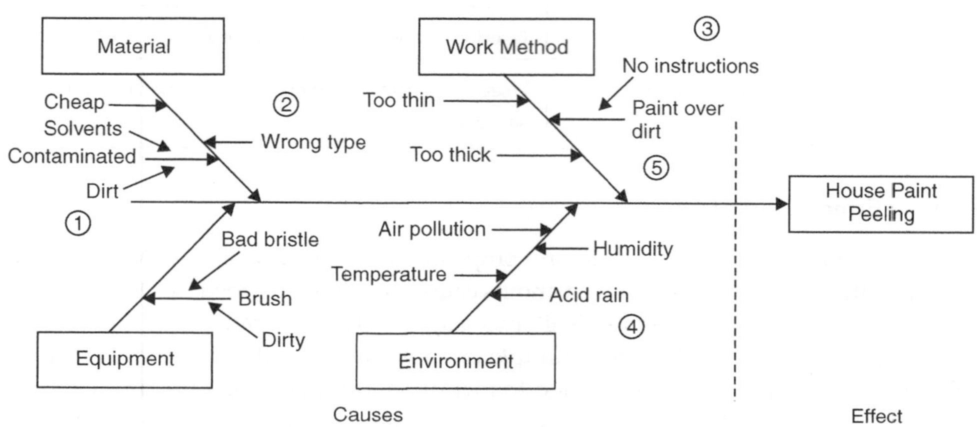

FIGURE 3.1 **Cause and Effect Diagram**

- Review the causes that are circled and ask, "Why is this cause?" Asking `why' will help get to the root cause of the problem.
- Reach an agreement on the most probable cause(s).

Essentials of Cause and Effect Diagram

- Be sure everyone agrees on the effect or problem statement before beginning.
- Be succinct.
- For each node, think what could be its causes. Add them to the tree.
- Pursue each line of causality back to its root cause.
- Consider grafting relatively empty branches on to others.
- Consider splitting up overcrowded branches.
- Consider which root causes are most likely to merit further investigation.

Uses of Cause and Effect Diagram

- It identifies the potential causes of a problem or issue in an orderly way (example: Why has the membership in the band decreased? Why isn't the phone being answered on time? Why is the production process suddenly producing so many defects?)
- It summarizes the major causes under four categories (example: people, machines, methods and, materials or policies, procedures, people and plant).

3.3.3 Histogram

The first statistical SPC technique is the histogram. It describes the variation in the process by the figure. The histogram graphically estimates the process capability and, if desired, the relationship to the specifications and the nominal (target).

A histogram is a specialized type of bar chart. Individual data points are grouped together in classes, so that you can get an idea of how frequently data in each class occur in the data set. High bars indicate more points in a class and low bars indicate less point.

Histograms provide a simple, graphical view of accumulated data, including its dispersion and central tendency. In addition to the ease with which they can be constructed, histograms provide the easiest way to evaluate the distribution of data. Two techniques are needed to accomplish this summarization of data. They are graphical and analytical.

The strength of a histogram is that it provides an easy-to-read picture of the location and variation in a data set.

Types of Histograms

There are five types of histograms based on five types of distributions. Each distribution type indicates a different type of behaviour. The various types of distributions are

(*a*) **Bell-shaped distribution:** Symmetrical shape with a peak in middle representing a normal distribution.

(*b*) **Double-peaked distribution:** Two normal distributions with two peaks in middle indicating more than one distribution at work.

(*c*) **Plateau distribution**: Flat top, no distinct peak and tails indicating more than one distribution at work.

(*d*) **Comb distribution:** Alternative peaks showing possible errors in data collection and analysis.

(*e*) **Skewed distribution:** A symmetrical shape positively or negatively skewed-usually reflecting limits in the specification on one side.

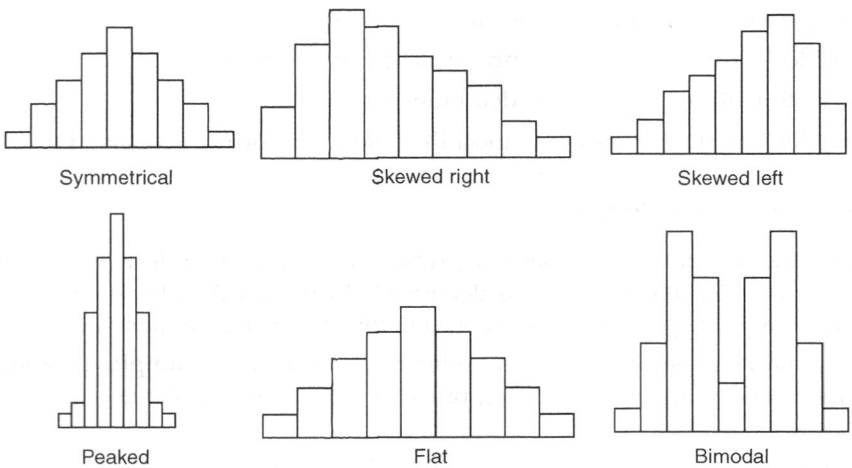

FIGURE 3.2 **Types of Histogram**

Disadvantages

- Histograms can be manipulated to show different pictures. If too few or too many bars are used the histogram can be misleading. This is an area which requires some judgement and, perhaps, some experimentation based on the analyst's experience.
- Histograms can also obscure the time differences among data sets.

3.3.4 Pareto Diagram

Alfredo Pareto (1848–1923) conducted extensive studies of the distribution of wealth in Europe. He concluded that a fairly consistent minority-about 20 per cent-of people controlled the large majority-about 80 per cent-of a society's wealth. This same distribution has been observed in other areas and has been termed as the 'Pareto Effect'. The Pareto Effect even operates in quality improvement: 80 per cent of the problems usually stem from 20 per cent of the causes. Pareto charts are used to display the Pareto principle in action, arranging data so that the few vital factors that cause most of the problems reveal themselves. Concentrating improvement efforts on these few will have a greater impact and be more cost-effective.

Pareto charts are extremely useful because they can be used to identify factors that have the greatest cumulative effect on the system, and, thus, screen out the less significant factors in an analysis. Ideally, his allows the user to focus attention on a few important factors in a process.

Steps in Constructing a Pareto Chart with an Example

(*a*) Determine the categories of problems or causes to be compared. Organise the problems or causes into a list of eight or fewer categories.

(*b*) Select a standard unit of measurement and the time period to be studied. It can be a measure of how often something occurs (defects, errors, cost overruns, etc.); frequencies of reasons cited in surveys as the cause of a certain problem; or a specific measurement of volume or size. The time period to be studied should be a reasonable length of time to collect the data.

(*c*) Collect and summarise the data. Create a three-column table under the heading of 'error or problem category', 'frequency', and 'percent of total'. In the 'error or problem category' column list the categories of problems or causes previously identified. In the 'frequency' column, write the totals for each of the categories over the designated period of time. In the 'percent of total' column, divide each number in the 'frequency' column by the total number of measurements.

(*d*) Create the framework for the horizontal and vertical axes of the Pareto chart. The horizontal axis will be the categories of problems or causes in a descending order with the most frequently occurring category on the far left (or at the beginning of the horizontal line). There will be two vertical axes-one on the far left and one on the far right. The vertical axis on the far left point will indicates the frequency for each of the categories. Scale it so the value at the top of the axis is slightly higher than the highest frequency number. The vertical axis on the far right will represent the percentage scale and should be scaled so that the point for the number of occurrences on the left matches with the corresponding percentage on the right.

(*e*) Plot the bars on the Pareto chart. Using a bar graph format, draw the corresponding bars in decreasing height from left to right using the frequency scale on the left vertical axis. To plot the cumulative percentage line, place a dot above each bar at a height corresponding to the scale on the right vertical axis. Then connect these dots from left to right, ending with the 100 percent point at the top of the right vertical axis.

(*f*) Interpret the Pareto chart. Use common sense just because a certain problem occurs most often doesn't necessarily mean it demands your greatest attention. Investigate all angles to help solve the problems like what makes the biggest difference? What will it cost to correct the problems? What will it cost if we don't correct this problem?

Uses of Pareto Diagram

(*a*) A Pareto chart is used for focusing on critical issues by ranking them in order of importance and frequency (example: Which course causes the most difficulty for students? Which problem with product X is most significant to our customers?)

(*b*) It prioritizes problems or causes to efficiently initiate problem-solving (example: Which discipline problems should be tackled first? What is the most frequent complaint by parents regarding the school? Solution of which production problem will improve quality most?)

(*c*) It analyses problems or causes by different groupings of data (example: By programme, by teacher, by school building, by machine, by team).

(*d*) It analyses the before and after impact of changes made in a process (example: What is the most common complaint of parents before and after the new principal was hired? Has the initiation of a quality improvement programme reduced the number of defects?)

3.3.5 Check Sheets

The main purpose of check sheets is to ensure that the data is collected carefully and accurately by operating personnel. Data should be collected in such a manner that it can be quickly and easily used and analyzed. The form of the check sheet is individualized for each solution and is designed by the project team. The figure shows a check sheet for paint nonconformities for bicycles.

Whenever possible, check sheets are also designed to show location. For example the check sheet for bicycle paint nonconformities could show an outline of a bicycle. Creativity plays a major role in the design of a check sheet. It should be user-friendly and whenever possible include information on time and location.

CHECK SHEET

Product : Bicycle 32 — Number inspected 2217

Nonconformity type	Check	Total
Blister	𝍸 𝍸 𝍸 𝍸 |	21
Light spray	𝍸 𝍸 𝍸 𝍸 𝍸 𝍸 𝍸 |||	38
Drips	𝍸 𝍸 𝍸 𝍸 ||	22
Overspray	𝍸 𝍸 |	11
Runs	𝍸 𝍸 𝍸 𝍸 𝍸 𝍸 𝍸 𝍸 𝍸 ||	47
Others	𝍸	5
	Total	144
Number Nonconforming	𝍸 |||	113

3.3.6 Scatter Diagram

Scatter diagrams are graphical tools that attempt to depict the influence that one variable has on the other. A common diagram of this type usually displays points representing the observed value of one variable corresponding to the value of another variable. This tool also shows the pattern of relationship between two variables. Examples of relationships are as follows:

- Cutting speed and tool life.
- Breakdowns and equipment age.

- Training and errors.
- Speed and gas mileage.
- Production speed and the number of defective parts.

A scatter diagram is used to investigate the possible relationship between two variables that relate to the same 'event'. A straight line of best fit (using the least squares method) is often included.

Steps in Constructing a Scatter Diagram

- Collect two pieces of data (a pair of numbers) on a student, process or product. Create a summary table of the data.
- Draw a diagram labeling the horizontal and vertical axes. It is common that the 'cause' variable is labeled the horizontal (X) axis and the 'effect' variable be labeled the vertical (Y) axis. The values should increase up the vertical scale and towards the right on the horizontal scale. The scale on both the X and Y axes should be able to include both the largest and the smallest X and Y values in the table.
- Plot the data pairs on the diagram by placing a dot at the intersection of the X and Y coordinates for each data pair.
- Interpret the scatter diagram for direction and strength.

Uses of Scatter Diagram

(*a*) Validating 'hunches' about a cause-and-effect relationship between types of variables (examples: I wonder if students who spend more time watching TV have higher or lower average GPAs? Is there a relationship between the production speed of an operator and the number of defective parts made' is there a relationship between typing speed in WPM and errors made?)

(*b*) Displaying the direction of the relationship (positive, negative, etc.) (Examples: Will test scores increase or decrease if the students spend more time in study hall'? Will the increasing assembly line speed increase or decrease the number of defective parts? Do faster typists make more or fewer typing errors?)

(*c*) Displaying the strength of the relationship (examples: How strong is the relationship between the measured IQ and grades earned in chemistry? How strong is the relationship between the assembly line speed and the number of defective parts produced,'? How strong is the relationship between typing faster and the number of typing errors made?)

3.3.7 Control Chart

A control chart is a statistical device principally used for the study and control of repetitive processes. Walter A. Shewart, its originator, suggested that control chart may serve, firstly, to define the goal of standard for the process that the management might strive to attain; secondly, it may be used as an instrument to attain that goal; and thirdly it may serve as a means of judging whether the goal has been achieved. Thus, it is an instrument to be used in specification, production and inspection.

A control chart is essentially a graphic device for presenting data so as to directly reveal the frequency and extent of variations from established standards or goals. Control charts are simple to construct and easy to interpret, and they tell the manager at a glance, whether or not the process is in control, *i.e.*, within the tolerance limits. A control chart consists of three horizontal lines:

(*i*) A central line (CL) to indicate the desired standard or level of the process;

(*ii*) Upper control limit (UCL); and

(*iii*) Lower control limit (LCL).

The outline of a control chart is given below:

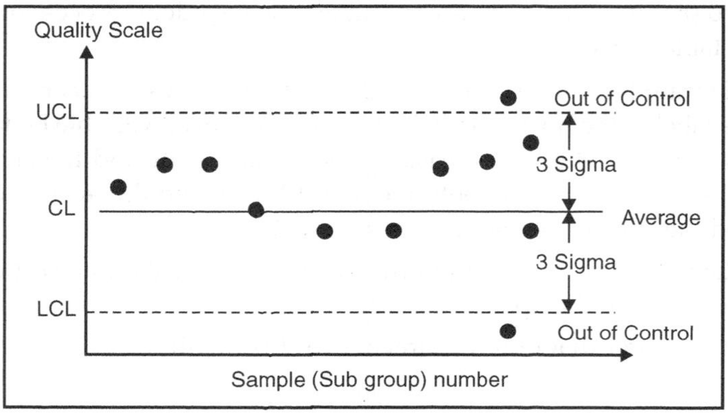

FIGURE 3.3 **Control Chart**

From time to time, a sample is taken and the data are plotted on the graph. So long as the sample points fall within the upper and lower control limits, there is nothing to worry as in such a case the variation between the samples is attributed to chance or unknown causes.

It is only when a sample point falls outside the control limits that it is considered to be a danger signal indicating that assignable causes are bringing about variations. Thus, there is no wastage of time and money in an effort to find the reason for random variation but as soon as an assignable cause is apparent, necessary corrective action is taken.

Thus, generally, if all dots are found between the upper and lower control limits, it is assumed that the process is "in control" and only chance causes are present. However, sometimes dots are found arranged in some peculiar way. Although they appear between the control limits, a substantial number of successive dots may be located on the same side of the central line or successive dots may follows a definite path leading towards the upper or lower control limit. Such patterns of dots within control limit should also be considered as danger signals which may indicate a change in the production process. Thus, control charts are not only watched for points falling outside the control limits, they are also scrutinized for unusual patterns suggesting trouble.

How to set up the Control Limits?

The basis of control chart is the setting up of upper and lower control limits. These limits are used as a basis for judging the significance of the quality variations from sample to sample, lot to lot or from time to time. The moment a point falls outside these limits, it is taken to be a danger signal. The control limits serve as a guide for action and, therefore, they are also referred to as action limits. Control limits are established by computation based upon:

(*i*) Data covering past and current production records; and

(*ii*) Statistical formulae whose reliability has been proved in practice.

Although, the nature of the control problem does not permit standardizing precise and inflexible rules for computing control limits that will be found suited to all of the various conditions that may be encountered in actual practice, it has been found possible to develop certain general procedures on the basis of experience that will cover a wide range of industrial applications.

In most control problems, it had been found satisfactory to place the control limits above and below the grand average of the statistical measures ($\overline{X}$, σ, R, etc.) that is being plotted at distances of three times a computed value, commonly designated as the "sigma" limits.* The logic of drawing 3 σ limits is that in case of a normal distribution, $3\ \overline{X} \neq 3\ \sigma$ covers 99.73 percent of the items. In other words, occurrence of events beyond the limits of ($\overline{X} \neq 3\ \sigma$), provided the events lie on a normal curve, is on the whole nearly 3 out of 1,000 events an extremely remote chance under normal circumstances. Hence, if points fall outside 3 sigma limits they indicate the presence of some assignable causes all is not due to random causes. It should be noted that if points fall outside 3 sigma limits, there is a good reason for confidence that they point out to some factor contributing to quality variation that can be identified.

The selection of standard value (of $\overline{X}$, σ, R, etc.) is probably the most basic problem encountered in setting up a control procedure. The primary aim is not just to get control, but to get control at a satisfactory level. A satisfactory selection depends fundamentally upon the needs of the buyer or user as defined by his specifications. Any questions of cost of production and capability of manufacturing process must, of course, also be taken into account in deciding on a level that will be economical from an average point of view.

Setting up a Control Procedure

In establishing basic procedures for the operation of a quality control programme, the manufacturer must take the following preliminary steps:

1. Select the quality characteristics that are to be controlled (including the limits of variation).
2. Analyse the production process to determine the kind and location of probable causes of irregularities.
3. Determine how the inspection data are to be collected and recorded, and how they are to be subdivided.
4. Choose the statistical measures that are to be used in the charts.

3.4 STATISTICAL FUNDAMENTALS

3.4.1 Introduction

- Statistics is defined as the science that deals with the collection, tabulation, analysis interpretation, and presentation of quantitative data.
- Each division is dependent on the accuracy and completeness of the preceding one.
- Data may be collected by a technician by measuring the tensile strength of a plastic part or an operator using a check sheet.
- It may be tabulated by simple paper-and-pencil technique or by the use of a computer. The final results are interpreted and presented to assist in the making of decisions concerning quality.

There are two principal analytical methods of describing a collection of data. They are measures of central tendency and measures of dispersion.

3.4.2 Measures of Central Tendency

A measure of central tendency of a distribution is a numerical value that describes the central Position of the data or how the data tend to build up in the center. There are three measures in common use in quality:

- The average.
- The median.
- The mode.

The average is the sum of the observations divided by the number of observations. It is the most common measure of central tendency and is represented by the equation.

$$\overline{X} = \frac{\sum_{i=1}^{n} X_i}{n}$$

where $\overline{X}$ = average and is read as "X bar"

n = number of observed values

X_i = observed value

Σ = sum of

Unless otherwise noted, $\overline{X}$ stands for the average of observed values, $\overline{X}_X$. The same equation is used to find

$\overline{\overline{X}}$ or $\overline{X}_{\overline{X}}$ — average of average

$\overline{R}$ — average of ranges

$\overline{P}$ — average of proportions, etc.

Another measure of central tendency is the median. Median is defined as the value that divides a series of ordered observations so that the number of items above it is equal to the number below it. Two situations are possible; when the number in the series is odd and when the series is even. When the number in the series is odd, the median is the mid point of the values, provided the data are ordered. Thus, the ordered set of numbers 3, 4, 5, 6, 8, 8, 10 has a median of 6. when the number in the series is even, 3, 4, 5, 6, 8, 8 has a median that is the average of 5 and 6 which is 5.5.

The mode is the value that occurs with the greatest frequency. It is possible for the mode to be nonexistent in a series of numbers 3, 3, 4, 5, 5, 5, 7 has a mode of 5.

3.4.3 Measures of Dispersion

A second tool of statistics is composed of the measure of dispersion which describes how the data are spread out or scattered on each side of the central value. Measures of dispersion and measure of central tendency are both needed to describe a collection of data. There are two measures of dispersion. They are range and standard deviation.

(*a*) **Range:** One of the measures of the dispersion is the range, which for a series of number is the difference between the largest and the smallest values of observations and it is expressed by the equation

$$R = X_h - X_l$$

where R = range

X_h = highest observation in a series

X_l = lowest observation in a series.

(*b*) **Standard Deviation:** The other measure of the dispersion used in quality is the standard deviation. It is a numerical value in the units of the observed values that measures the spreading tendency of the data. A larger standard deviation shows greater variability of the data than does a small standard deviation and it is represented by the equation

$$s = \sqrt{\frac{\sum_{i=1}^{n} (X_i - \overline{X})^2}{n-1}}$$

where s = sample standard deviation

X_l = observation value

$\overline{X}$ = average

n = number of observed values

Unless otherwise noted, s stands for $s_{X'}$ the sample standard deviation of observed values. The same equation is used to find

$s_{\overline{X}}$ = sample standard deviation of averages

s_p = sample standard deviation of proportions

s_s = sample standard deviation of standard deviations, etc.

3.5 POPULATION AND SAMPLE

Population: The population is the whole collection of data. When the averages, standard deviations and other measures are computed from the samples, they are referred to as statistics.

A population in statistics is used to refer to any collection of individuals or of their attributes or of results of operations. It is also known as Universe. There are two types of population. They are finite and infinite population.

A population containing a finite number of individuals or members is called a finite population. For example the population of ages of 40 students in a class.

A population containing an infinite number of individuals or members is known as infinite population. For example, the population of pressures at various points in the atmosphere.

Sample: A part or small section selected from the population is called sample. The process of such selection is called sampling.

Because of the composition of samples will fluctuate the computed statistics will be larger or smaller than their true population values or parameters. Parameters are considered to be fixed reference values or the best estimate of these values available at a particular time. Sampling is necessary when it may be impossible to measure the entire population.

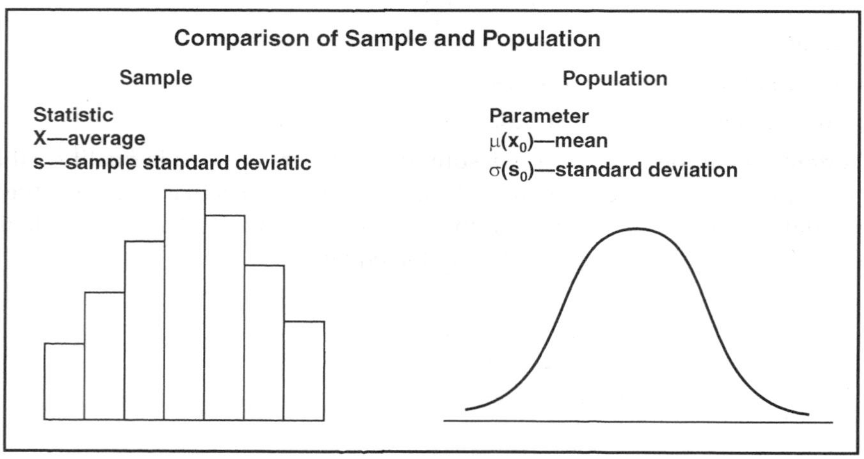

3.6 NORMAL CURVE

The normal curve is the frequency curve. It is also known as Gaussian curve and probability curve.

Although there are as many different populations as there are conditions, they can be described by a general few types.

The normal curve is a symmetrical, unmodal bell-shaped distribution with the mean, median, and mode having the same value.

Most of the variation in natural and in industry, it follows the frequency distribution of the normal curves. For example, the variation in the height of the human beings, the variations in dimension of an automobile product, the life period of tubes, bulbs and valves.

The normal curve is such a good description of the variations that occur to most quality characteristics in industry that it is the basis for many quality control techniques.

There is a definite relationship among the mean, the standard deviation and the normal curve. Figure 3.4 shows three normal curves with different mean value and the only change in the location.

The normal distribution is fully defined by the population mean and population standard deviation.

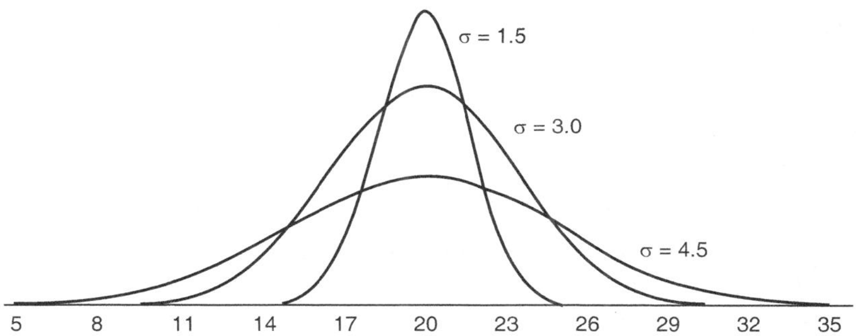

FIGURE 3.4 **Normal Curves with Different SD but Identical Means**

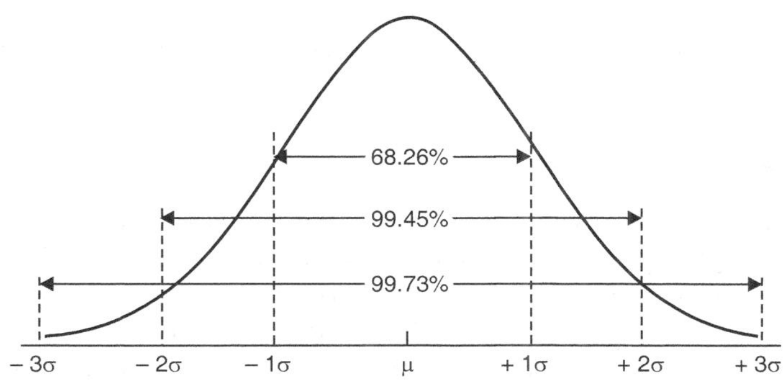

FIGURE 3.5 **Percent of Values is included between Certain Values of the SD**

3.7 INTRODUCTION TO CONTROL CHARTS

Variation

The variation may be quite large and easily noticeable such as the height of human beings, or the variation may be very small, such as the weights of fiber tipped pens or the shapes of snowflakes.

When variations are very small it may appear that items are identical and however, precision instruments will show differences.

There are three categories of variations in piece part production:

- Within piece variation is illustrated by the surface roughness of a piece, wherein one portion of the surface is rougher than another portion or the width of one end of a keyway varies from the other end.
- Piece to piece variation occurs among pieces produced at the same time. Thus, the light intensity of four consecutive light bulbs produced from a machine will be different.
- Time-to -time variation is illustrated by the differences in product produced at different times of the day. Thus product produced at the early morning is different from that produced later in the day, or as a cutting tool wears, the cutting characteristics change.

Categories of variations for other types of processes such as continuous and batch are not exactly the same: however, the concept is similar.

Variation is present in every process due to a combination of the equipment, materials, environment and operator.

The first source of variation is the equipment. This source includes not only tool were, machine vibration but also work holding-device positioning and hydraulic and electrical fluctuation.

The second source of variation is the material, because variation occurs in the finished product, it must also occur in the raw material. Such quality characteristics as tensile strength, ductility, thickness, porosity, moisture contents.

The third source of variation is the environment. Temperature, light, radiation, particle size, pressure, and humidity all can contribute to variation in the product.

The fourth is the operator. This source of variation includes the method by which the operator performs the operation. The operator's physicals and emotional well being also contribute to the variation.

3.7.1 Control Chart

Control chart is a graphical representation of measured actual process performance relating to computed control limits. It deducts the variation in processing and warns if there is any deviation from the specified tolerance limits. The control chart is being used in solving problem related to process stability and improvement of capability by reducing the variability in the process adopted. It is used for controlling the characteristics of any kind of processes in order to improve the quality of the product.

Objectives of Control Chart

- To provide the basis for taking decisions related to the acceptance or rejection of products being manufactured.
- To determine and eliminate the assignable causes of variations in a process.

- To constantly monitor a process to determine whether the process is controlled statically or not.
- To evaluate process stability and to decide when to adjust the process.
- To improve the existing production procedures by analyzing the capability of the machine and the process.

Types of Control Chart

Control chart are classified into two types. They are:

- Control chart for variables
- Control chart for attributes.

Control charts for variables

The quality characteristics which can be measured and expressed in specific units of measurements are called variables. For example, dimensions, physical characteristics like tensile strength, density etc.

Two types of control charts are popular

1. Mean ($\overline{x}$) – Chart
2. Range (R) – Chart

$\overline{\text{X}}$-Chart

It based on the distribution of sample means. It is used to determine, it variation in a product dimension are random and to detect assignable variation.

Formula for fixing the control limit for $\overline{x}$ chart is

Upper Control Limit, $UCL_{\overline{X}} = \overline{\overline{X}} + AR$ (or) $UCL_{\overline{X}} = \overline{\overline{X}} + A_2R$

Lower Control Limit, $LCL_{\overline{X}} = \overline{\overline{X}} - A\overline{R}$ (or) $LCL_{\overline{X}} = \overline{\overline{X}} - A_2\overline{R}$

where $\overline{\overline{X}}$ = Mean of mean, $\overline{\overline{X}} = \dfrac{\sum \overline{x}}{N}$

$\overline{R}$ = Mean of Range

A/A_2 = Constant. The value of A/A_2 for different sample size is given in table.

R-Chart

R-Chart is used to show the variability (or) dispersion of the quality produced by a given process. It is also called σ-Chart. The R-Chart is generally presented along with the $\overline{X}$ Chart.

Formula for fixing the R-Chart is

$$\text{Upper Control Limit} = UCL_R = R + 3\sigma_R = B\overline{R} \text{ (or) } UCL_R = D_4\overline{R}$$

$$\text{Lower Control Limit} = LCL_R = R - 3\sigma_R = C\overline{R} \text{ (or) } LCL_R = D_3\overline{R}$$

where,

R = Range of a sample observation

σ_R = Standard Deviation of R

B (or) D_4 and C (or) D_3 = are constant. The values of B/D_4 and C/D_3 for different sample size are given in able.

Different Control Charts for Variables

Type	Central Line	Central Limits	Comments
$\overline{X}$ and S	$\overline{X}$	$UCL_{\overline{X}} = \overline{\overline{X}} + A_3\overline{S}$ $LCL_{\overline{X}} = \overline{\overline{X}} - A_3\overline{S}$	Use when more sensitivity is desired than R, when $n > 10$, and when data are collected automaticaly.
	$\overline{S}$	$UCL_S = B_4\overline{S}$ $LCL = B_3SL$	
Moving average, $M\overline{X}$ and moving range, MR	$\overline{\overline{X}}$	$UCL_{\overline{X}} = \overline{\overline{X}} + A_2\overline{R}$ $LCL_{\overline{X}} = \overline{\overline{X}} - A_2\overline{R}$	Use when only one observation is possible at a time. Data needn't be normal.
	$\overline{R}$	$UCL_R = D_4\overline{R}$ $UCL_R = D_3\overline{R}$	
X and moving R	$\overline{X}$	$UCL_{\overline{X}} = \overline{X} + 2.660\overline{R}$ $LCL_X = \overline{X} - 2.660\overline{R}$ $LCL_R = 3.276\overline{R}$	Use when only one observation is possible at a time and the data are nromal.
	$\overline{R}$	$LCL_R = (0)\,\overline{R}$	Equations are based on a moving range of two.
Median and Range	Md_{md}	$UCL_{Md} = MD_{Md} + A_5\,R_{Md}$ $LCL_{Md} = Md_{Md} - A_5\,R_{Md}$	Use when process in a maintenance mode. Benefits are less arithmetic and simplicity.
	R_{md}	$UCL_R = D_6\,R_{Md}$ $LCL_R = D_5\,R_{Md}$	

Control Charts for Attributes

Attribute: Attributes are such parameters which are not amenable to measurement. For example visually suspected items such as colour, missing parts, scratches and damages, air bubbles etc. These are identified either by their presence or absence.

An attributes refers to those quality characteristics that conform to specifications or do not conform, to specifications. There are two types of control charts for attributes.

The term nonconforming unit is used to describe a unit of product or service containing at least one non conformity. Defective is analogous to defect and is appropriate for use when a unit of product or service is evaluated in terms of usage rather than conformance to specifications. In this section we are using the terms non conformity and nonconforming unit. This practice avoids the confusion and misunderstanding that occurs with defect and defective in product-liability lawsuits. Nonconformities such as missing parts, in correct color, and so on, are not measurable, and a variable control chart is not applicable. In this situation, attribute control charts will be used.

There are two different groups of control charts for attributes. One group of charts is for nonconforming units.

- A proportion, P-chart shows the proportion nonconforming in a sample or subgroup.
- The proportion is expressed as a fraction or a percent. Another chart in the group is for number nonconforming is *np*-chart.

Another group of charts is for nonconformities.

- C chart shows the count of non-conformities in an inspected unit such as an automobile, bolt of cloth, or roll of paper.
- Another closely-related chart is the U chart, which is for the count of nonconformities per unit.

Objectives of Attribute Charts

The objectives of attribute charts are to:

- Determine the average quality level. Knowledge of the quality average is essential as a benchmark. This information provides the process capability in terms of attributes.
- Bring to the attention of management, any change in the average. Changes, either increasing or decreasing, become significant once the average quality is known.
- Improve the product quality. In this regard, an attribute chart can motivate operating and management personnel to initiate ideas for quality improvement. The chart will tell whether the idea is an appropriate or inappropriate one. A continual and relentless effort must be made to improve the quality.
- Evaluate the quality performance of operating and management personnel. Supervisors should be evaluated by a chart for nonconforming units.
- Suggest places to use $\overline{X}$ and R charts. Even though the cost of computing and charting $\overline{X}$ and R charts is more than that of charts for attributes, they are much more sensitive to variations and are more helpful in diagnosing causes. In other words, the attribute chart suggests the source of difficulty, and $\overline{X}$ and R charts find the cause.
- Determine acceptance criteria of a product before shipment to the customer. Knowledge of attributes provides management with information on whether or not to release an order.

Use of the Chart

The general procedures that apply to variable control charts also apply to the p chart. The first step in the procedure is to determine the use of the control chart. The p chart is used for data that consist of the proportion of the number of occurrences of an event to the total number of occurrences. It is used in quality control to report the proportion non conforming in a product, quality characteristic, or group of quality characteristics. As such, the proportion nonconforming is the ratio of the number nonconforming in a sample or subgroup to the total number in the sample or subgroup.

Control Charts for Attributes

Control charts for attributes monitor the number of defects or fraction defect rate present in the sample. In this regard two types of charts are used. They are:

P-Chart

C-Chart

P-Chart

This is the percentage or proportion of defectives. It is based on binomial distribution. The main purpose is

- *To discover the average proportion of non conforming articles or parts submitted for inspection over a period of time.*
- *To bring to the management attention, if there is any charges in average quality level.*

Formula for Control Limits are as follows.

$$UCL_P = \bar{p} + 3\sqrt{\frac{\bar{p}\bar{q}}{n}} = \bar{p} + 3\sigma\,\bar{p}$$

$$LCL_P = \bar{p} - 3\sqrt{\frac{\bar{p}\bar{q}}{n}} = \bar{p} - 3\sigma\,\bar{p}$$

where, P = Process percentage defective of a sample

= No. of defective items in a sample)/n

$\bar{p}$ = Process mean percent defectives = $\frac{\sum P}{k}$

n = Sample size

k = Number of Samples

$\sigma_{\bar{p}}$ = SD of percent defectives = $\sqrt{\frac{pq}{n}}$

C-Chart

It is used for controlling the number of defects per sample unit. It is used where chances of defects are high while occurrence is small. Usually, the sample size is considered to be one (n=1). The Control limits of this chart are based on Poisson distribution.

Uses:

The control the number of non- conforming rivets in an aircraft using.

The control the number of imperfection observed in a galvanized sheet.

The control the number of surface imperfections on a large casting like gear blank, which is used to kiln in cement plant.

To control the number of defects in final assembles like TV, Radio, Computer, etc...

The formula for control limit are given below.

$$UCL^{\bar{c}} = \bar{C} + 3\sqrt{\bar{C}}$$

$$LCL^{\bar{c}} = \bar{C} - 3\sqrt{\bar{C}}$$

Different types of Control Charts for Attributes

Type	Central Line	Control Limits	Comments
p	$\bar{p}$	$\text{UCL} = \bar{p} + 3\sqrt{\frac{\bar{p}(1-\bar{p})}{n}}$ $\text{LCL} = \bar{p} - 3\sqrt{\frac{\bar{p}(1-p)}{n}}$	Use for nonconforming units with constant or variable sample size.
np	$\overline{np}$	$\text{UCL} = \overline{np} + 3\sqrt{\overline{np}\,(1-\bar{p})}$ $\text{LCL} = \overline{np} - 3\sqrt{\overline{np}\,(1-\bar{p})}$	Use for nonconforming units, where np is the number nonconforming. The simple size must be constant.
c	$\bar{c}$	$\text{UCL} = \bar{c} + 3\sqrt{\bar{c}}$ $\text{LCL} = \bar{c} - 3\sqrt{\bar{c}}$	Use for the nonconformities within a unit where c is the count of nonconformities. The sample size is one inspected unit *i.e.*, a case of 24 cans.
u	$\bar{u}$	$\text{UCL} = \bar{u} + 3\sqrt{\frac{\bar{u}}{n}}$ $\text{LCL} = \bar{u} - 3\sqrt{\frac{\bar{u}}{n}}$	Use for nonconformities within a unit where u is the count of nonconformities per unit. The sample size can vary.

Subgroup Size and Method

The data that are plotted on the control chart consist of groups of items called rational subgroups. It is important to understand that data collected in a random manner do not qualify as rational. A rational subgroup is one in which the variation within the group is due only to chance causes. This within-subgroup variation is used to determine the control limits. Variation between subgroups is used to evaluate long-term stability. Subgroup samples are selected from product or a service produced at one instant of time or as close to that instant as possible, such as four consecutive parts from a machine or four documents from a tray.

Decisions on the size of the sample or subgroup require a certain amount of empirical judgment however, some helpful guidelines are:

- As the subgroup size increases, the control limits become closer to the central value, which make the control chart more sensitive to small variations in the process average.

- As the subgroup size increases, the inspection cost per subgroup increases.
- Does the increased cost of larger subgroups justify the greater sensitivity?
- When costly and/or destructive testing is used and the item is expensive, a small sub group size of two or three is necessary, because it will minimize the destruction of expensive product.
- Because of the ease of computation, a sample size of five is quite common in industry; however, when inexpensive electronic hand calculators are used, this reason is no longer valid.

3.8 PROCESS CAPABILITY

Process capability is the ability of the process to produce uniform products in order to meet the design specifications. Specifations are the allowable variation in the size of the products. These specifications or tolerance limits are established by design engineer to meet a particular function, whereas control limits are established as the function of average.

Figure shows that the location of the specifications is optional and is not related to any of the other features in the figure. The control limits, process spread (process capability), distribution of averages, and distribution of individual values are interdependent.They are determined by the process, whereas the specifications have an optional location. Control charts cannot determine if the process is meeting specifications.

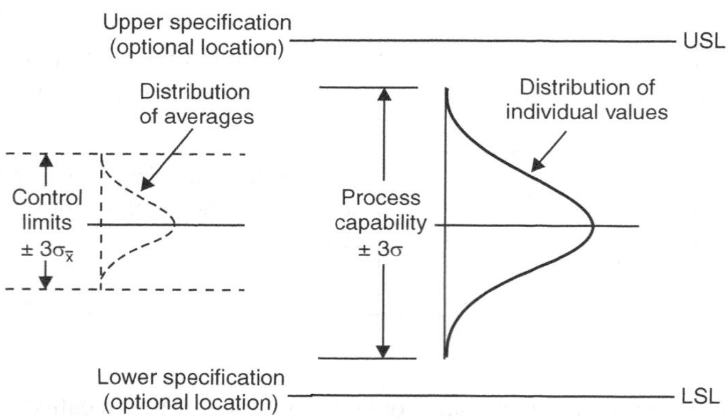

FIGURE 3.6 **Relationship of Limits, Specification, and Distributions**

The true process capability cannot be determined until the $\overline{X}$ and R charts have achieved the optimal quality improvement without a substantial investment for new equipment or equipment modification. When the process is in statistical control, process capability is equal to six sigma, where $\sigma = R_0/d_2$ is a factor from Appendix Table.

It is frequently necessary to obtain the process capability by a quick method rather than by using the $\overline{X}$ and R charts. This method assumes the process is stable or in statistical control, which may or may not be the case.

The procedure is as follows

- Take 25 subgroups of size 4, for a total of 100 measurements.
- Calculate the range, for each subgroup.
- Calculate the average range.
- Calculate the estimate of the population standard deviation.
- The process capability will equal to 6σ.

Remember that this technique does not give the true process capability and should be used only if circumstances require its use. Also, more than 25 subgroups can be used to improve accuracy. Tolerance is the difference between the upper specification limit (USL) and the lower specifications limit (LSL). Process capability and the tolerance are combined to form a capability index, defined as

$$C_p = \frac{USL - LSL}{6s}$$

where $USL - LSL$ = upper specification – lower specification, or tolerance

C_p = capability index

6σ = process capability

If the capability index is greater than 1.00, the process is capable of meeting the specifications; if the index is less than 1.00, the process is not capable of meeting the specifications.

Because processes are continually shifting back and forth, a C_p value of 1.33 has become a defacto standard, and some organizations are using a 2.00 values. Using the capability index concept, we can measure quality, provided the process is centered. The larger the capability index, the better the quality. We should strive to make the capability index as large as possible. This result is accomplished by having realistic specifications and continual striving to improve the process capability. The capability index does not measure process performance in terms of the nominal or target value. This measure is accomplished using C_{pk} which is equal to

$$C_{pk} = \text{Min } \{[USL - \overline{X}] \text{ or } [\overline{X} - LSL]\}/3\sigma$$

A C_{pk} value of 1.00 is the de-facto standard, with some organizations using a value of 1.33. Following figures illustrate C_p and C_{pk} values for processes that are centered and also off centre by 1σ.

Quality professionals will use these eight items to improve the process. For example, if a C value is less than one, then corrective action must occur. Initially 100% inspection is necessary to eliminate non conformities one solution would be to increase the tolerance of the specifications. Another would be to work on the process to reduce the standard deviation or variability.

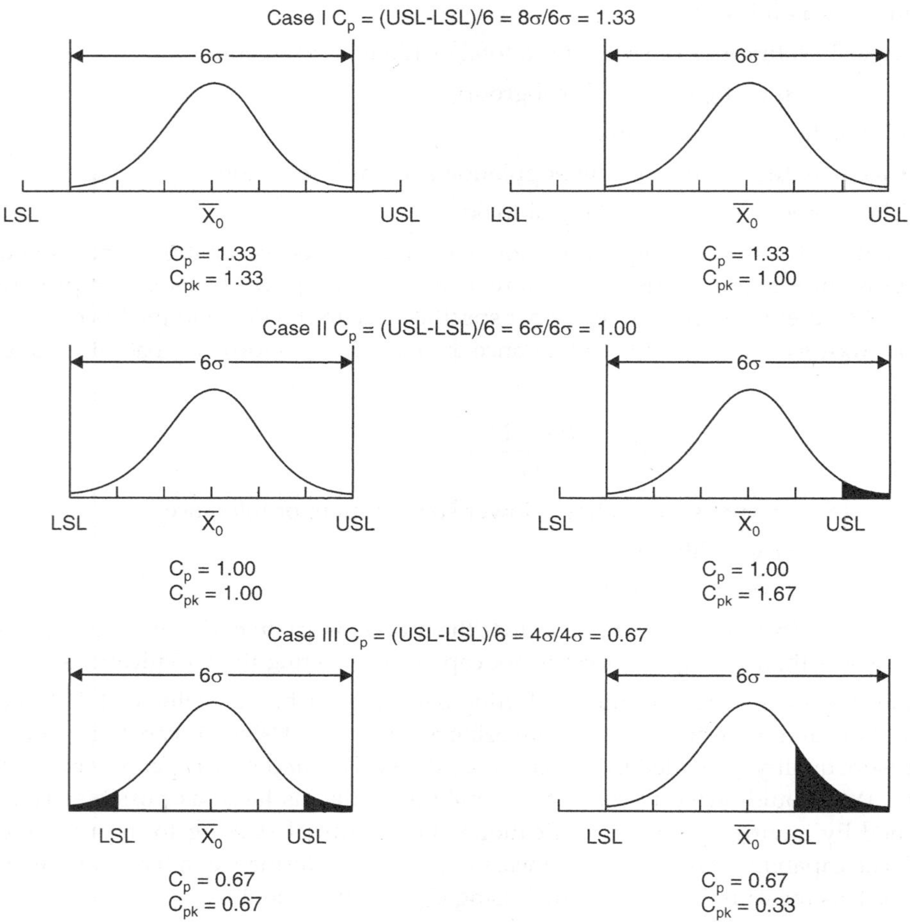

FIGURE 3.7 **C_p and C_{pk} Values for Three Different Situations**

3.9 SIX SIGMA

Introduction

Six sigma was started by Motorola in 1987, in its manufacturing division. Six sigma similar to zero defect, a philosophical benchmark or standard of excellence proposed by Philip Crosby. It provides a techniques and tools to improve the capability and reduce the defects in any process.

The six sigma strategy measures the degree to which any process, has deviated from its mean without causing errors in the operation. The various levels of sigma capability, defects, and cost of poor qualities are shown in the table.

Quality level	Defects per million parts produced	Cost of poor quality	Product status
1σ	6,90,000	40% – 70% of sales	Non competitive
2σ	3,08,537	30% – 40% of sales	
3σ	66,807	20% – 30% of sales	Industry average
4σ	6,210	15% – 20% of sales	
5σ	233	10% – 15% of sales	
6σ	3.4	Less than 10% of sales	World glass

In the above table, it is observed that, a if a company operates on two sigma level, around 30%–40% of sales is used up as a cost of poor quality and the defects are also more. *i.e.*, 6,90,000 defects per million part produced. On the other hand, the company operates on six sigma level, only 10–15% of sales is used up as cost of poor quality and the defects are very minimum *i.e.*, 3.4 defects per million parts produced. Therefore 6σ quality represents almost zero defects with world glass quality.

Steps Involved Achieving 6σ Concept

The following five steps which are involved in implementing 6σ concept. They are

(*a*) **Define:** The goal of an organization is defined to and set the policies and procedures and for identifying the customer requirements.

(*b*) **Measure:** The existing system is well measured for and displaying the data.

(*c*) **Analyse:** The gap between the current performance of the system and the aimed target is identified. These data are analysed and then improvement opportunities are determined.

(*d*) **Improve:** Planning and project management tools are improved to fill up the gap identified in the previous step. The present system is improved by adopting creativity to do things in a cheaper, better and faster manner.

(*e*) **Control:** After improving the system, it is very essential to control the system level parameters, in order to maintain the better outputs.

Finally the system is standardized by the way of communicating the benefits of the new system to the customers, employees and suppliers.

Advantages of Six Sigma

- It is used to indicate the extent to which a process can vary without causing errors in the operations.
- This approach aims to reduce the defects level into only few parts per million parts inspected. It aims to achieve zero defects product.
- It identifies and eliminates causes of defects in the process/operations. Hence the customer satisfaction with more return on investment to the organization.

- It provides extensive training to the project team and hence the cycle time is reduced with more profit.
- It is a strategic tool that aims to improve the process performance and maintains consistent quality of the process output.
- Six sigma principle and techniques are used in business, statistics and engineering. It improves the work system, training and the work environment.
- It decreases the cost of inspection and reduces the rework.

3.10 THE NEW SEVEN MANAGEMENT TOOLS

The "advanced" tools that are used to manage cross-functionality include the "seven new Quality Control Tools" also known as the "seven management and planning tools" or "seven MP tools".

How Were These New Seven Tools Developed?

A committee for developing QC tools, affiliated with the Osaka Base QC course of JUSE, was set up in April 1972 with the aim of developing QC techniques for use by managers and staff. Yoshinobu Nayatani headed this committee. In January 1977, the committee announced the results of its research in the form of a new set of methods called 'The Seven New QC Tools'.

- Affinity Diagram is also known as the KJ Method, which was developed by Kawakita Jiro.
- The Systematic or Tree Diagram is nothing new but an adaptation of the Functional Analysis System (FAST) Technique in value engineering.
- The Matrix diagram is an adaptation from the Feasibility Ranking Method Matrix of value engineering.
- PDPC diagram is an adaptation of the operations research methods.
- The Arrow Diagram is nothing but a derivative of PERT (Programme Evaluation and Review Technique) and CPM (Critical Path Methodology).
- The Matrix Data Analysis has its roots in the multivariate analysis method whose calculation is quite complex.

Following are the new seven management tools:

- Affinity Diagram
- Relations Diagram
- Tree Diagram
- Matrix Diagram
- Matrix Data Analysis Diagram
- Process Decision Programme Chart
- Arrow Diagram.

3.10.1 Affinity Diagram

The affinity diagram, also known as the KJ method, gets the name from its inventor, Kawakita Jiro. This is essentially a brainstorming method. It is based on group work in which every participant writes down his/her ideas which are, then, grouped and realigned by the subject matter. The affinity diagram is a very simple but powerful technique for grouping and understanding information, which gathers large amounts of intertwined verbal data (ideas, opinions, issues etc.). It organizes verbal data into groups based on natural relationships. Such information of distinct groups enable a meaningful picture to emerge, thereby making it feasible for further analysis and finding a solution to the problem.

Steps in Constructing an Affinity Diagram

(*a*) State the issue or problem to be explored. Start with a clear statement of the problem or goal and provide a time limit for the session. Usually, 45-60 minutes is sufficient.

(*b*) Brainstorm ideas for the issue or problem. Each participant should think of ideas and write them individually on index cards, sticky notes, or have a recorder to write them on a flip chart.

(*c*) Collect the cards or sticky notes, mix them and spread them out (or stick them) on a flat surface (*e.g.*, desk or wall). Index cards can easily be secured to a wall with a putty-type adhesive.

(*d*) Arrange the cards or sticky notes into related groups. Allow the participants to pick out cards that, a list related ideas for some 15 minutes and set them aside until all the cards are grouped.

(*e*) Create a title or heading for each grouping that best describes the theme of each group of cards.

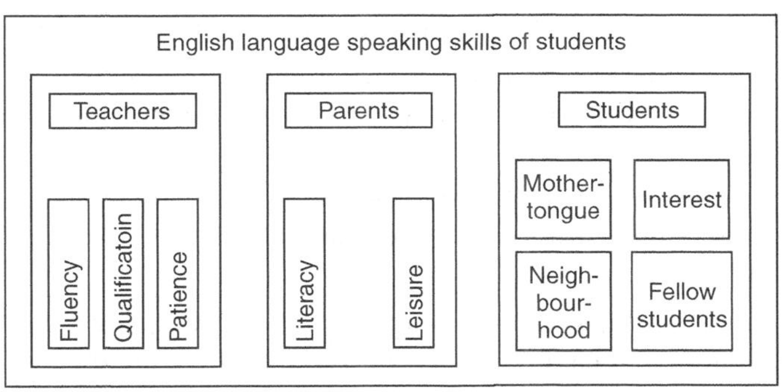

FIGURE 3.8 **Affinity Diagram**

Uses of Affinity Diagram

(*a*) It adds structure to a large or complicated issue (example: What are the issues relative to implementing a thematic approach to teaching? What are the central issues in the development of a new product?)

(*b*) It breaks down a complicated issue into broad categories (example: Which departments are more likely to implement TQM in this school? What are the major steps in the completion of a complex project?)

(*c*) It is used to reach an agreement on an issue or situation (example: Which direction should the school take to restructure its curriculum? How should a new product be marketed?)

When to use the Affinity Diagram?

- You can use the affinity diagram in a workshop environment when you want participants to work together in identifying, grouping and discussing issues.
- You can also use the tool when you have a large amount of information. For example, at the end of contextual enquiry when you may have hundreds or even thousands of individual notes.

3.10.2 Relations Diagram

Relations diagram, also known as ***interrelationship diagram***, is a tool for finding solutions to problems that have a complex causal relationship. This helps to untangle and find a logical relation among the intertwined causes and effects. It is a creative process, which allows for 'multi-directional' rather than 'linear' thinking.

An interrelations diagram is a graphical representation of all the factors in a complicated problem system or situation. It is typically used in conjunction with one of the other quality tools, particularly the affinity diagram. Frequently, the header card from the affinity diagram is used as the starting point for the interrelations diagram.

Steps in Constructing an Interrelations Diagram

(*a*) State clearly the issue or problem. Write it on a card and stick it on the centre of a board.

(*b*) Determine the factors related to the issue. Frequently, these will be the headers from a previously completed affinity diagram. Place the cards containing these factors in a circle around the issue card.

(*c*) Determine if cause-effect relationships exist between any of the cards. If so, draw an arrow from the 'cause' card to the 'effect' card. Do this for all cause/effect relationships that you can find.

(*d*) Analyse the relationships. Cards that have most arrows going from them tend to be the root causes, Cards that have most arrows going to them are the root effects.

Relations diagrams specify the relationships among things. More specifically, these diagrams are used to map and analyze problems where causes of the problem have complex interrelationships. In contrast to the Ishikawa diagram in which all the causes of a problem are assumed to be hierarchically decomposable, the relations diagram promotes the discovery of relationship among causes. In plain terms, this means that a single thing might influence two or more other things, a situation that cannot be easily shown in fishbone diagram. Consider the figure below which shows multiple relationships among the causes of specific problem. When teams work in a group to create relation diagrams, the 'card' or 'post-it note' technique can be used in which causes are specified by team members and arranged on a table or board and arrows drawn between cards or notes as needed to show the relationships.

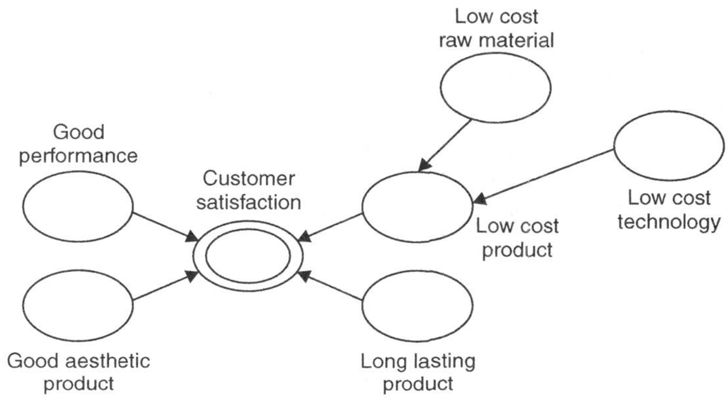

FIGURE 3.9 **Relations Diagram**

Uses of Interrelations Diagram

- The tool helps in identifying key or driver issues from a list of important issues.
- It helps in identifying the most important problems from a plethora, particularly when the number of problems exceeds the resources available to solve all of them.
- Identifying the root cause of existing problems.
- Identifying key factors needed to make a decision when there is insufficient information available to make a data-driven decision.

3.10.3 Tree Diagram

Systematic diagram or tree diagram is a technique for mapping out the full range of paths and tasks that need to be done to achieve a primary goal and related sub-goals. Such a diagram does not only reveal, simply and clearly the magnitude of the problem. It also helps to arrive at methods by which to achieve the results. In other words, it serves the purpose of developing the essential means to achieve an objective or goal.

A systematic diagram is a hierarchical graphic representation of the steps necessary to accomplish a goal or task. It is an application of a method originally developed for function analysis in value engineering.

Systematic diagrams can be divided into two types. They are

- The constituent-component-analysis diagram breaks down the main subject into basic elements and depicts their relationships to the objectives and the means of obtaining those objectives.
- The plan-development diagram systematically shows the means and procedures necessary to successfully implement a given plan.

Steps in Constructing a Systematic Diagram

- State the issue, problem or goal. Place this on a card on the left side of the board.
- Develop levels of events/tasks that must be accomplished to completely solve the problem or meet the goal. Typically, levels to the left are broad and as the levels are arranged to the right, they become more and more specific. Typically, events on the right side of the diagram are a prerequisite to those on the left. Analyze the completed diagram and assign tasks so the project can be completed.
- Once the systematic diagram is organized and completed, the tip nodes (those to the right in the figure) represent specific methods and actions. In this configuration, one can use a matrix diagram to priorities and organize the work to be done.

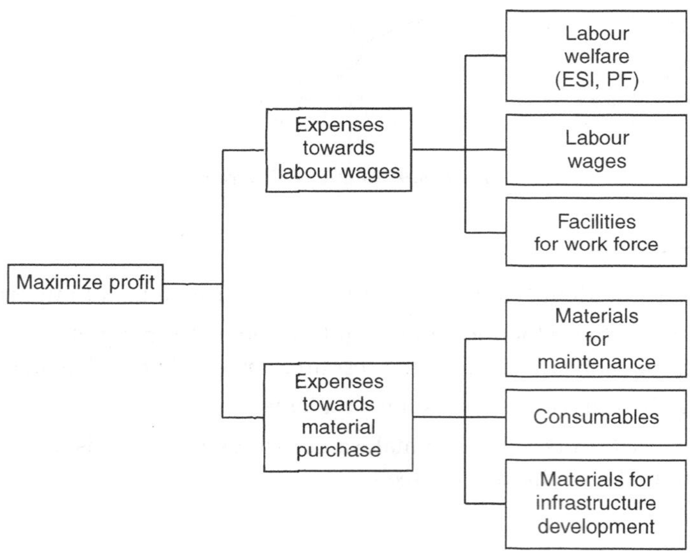

FIGURE 3.10 **Tree Diagram**

The main advantages of tree diagrams are as follows:

- They allow a system of strategies for solving a problem or means of achieving an objective to be developed systematically and logically, making it less likely that any essential items will be omitted.
- They facilitate agreement among group members. They are quite convincing because they identify and display clearly the strategies for solving a problem.
- It enables developing a sequence of steps that depend on each other and form the solution to a problem.
- It is used when it is known that the implementation of a task will be a complex matter.
- It is used when missing a key step in implementing the solution to a problem can lead to serious consequences.

Decision trees are useful in revealing the outcome and potential consequences of alternative decisions. They are particularly useful in situations where a series of decisions must be taken but which cannot easily be shown in a tabular form.

3.10.4 Matrix Diagram

A matrix diagram is a tool that is used to systematically organise information that must be compared on a variety of characteristics in order to make a comparison, selection or choice.

A matrix diagram consists of a number of columns and rows whose intersections are checked to find the nature and strength of the problem which help us to arrive at key ideas and analyse the relationship or its absence at the intersection. It also helps find an effective way of pursuing the problem-solving method. This enables conception of ideas on two-dimensional relationship bases. The intersection points are also called "idea conception points".

The matrix diagram method clarifies problematic spots through multi-dimensional thinking. This method identifies corresponding elements involved in a problem situation or event. These elements are arranged in rows and columns on a chart that shows the presence or absence of relationships among collected pairs of elements. Effective problem-solving is facilitated at the intersection points, also referred to as the idea conception points.

Steps in Constructing a Matrix Diagram

(*a*) Determine the factors that are important for making a correct selection.

(*b*) Select the type of matrix to be used. L-shaped matrices are used for two-factor comparisons, T-shaped for three-factor comparisons that display indirect and direct relationships, and Y-shaped are used for three-factor comparisons that show direct relationship only.

(*c*) Select the relationship symbols to be used.

(*d*) Complete the proper matrix using the appropriate factors and symbols.

(*e*) Examine the matrix and draw the appropriate conclusion.

Matrix-related Tools

On the basis of their pattern matrix diagrams are classified into five groups:

Sl.No.	Type of matrix	Description
1.	The L-type matrix	Comparison of two set of data.
2.	The T-type matrix	Comparison of two group of items with a core group of item.
3.	The Y-type matrix	Composes of three groups of items.
4.	The X-type matrix	Comparison of four sets of data which are related.
5.	The C-type matrix.	It compares three sets of data such as men, machine and materials in a company.

Industrial Applications of a Matrix Diagram

- It is often used in deploying quality requirements for counterpart (engineering) characteristics and then for production requirements.
- Establish idea conception points for the development and improvement of system products.
- Achieve quality deployment in product materials.
- Establish and strengthen the quality assurance system by linking certified levels of quality with various control functions.
- Reinforce and improve the efficiency of the quality evaluation system.
- Pursue the causes of non-conformities in the manufacturing process.
- Establish strategies about the product mix by evaluating the relationships between the products and market situations.

Uses of Matrix Diagram

(*a*) The tool is used for assigning tasks to complete a project.

(*b*) It is also used to make comparisons between competing alternatives that involve multiple characteristics.

(*c*) It enables prioritising combinations of new and old activities that maximise the number of total objectives met.

3.10.5 Matrix Data Analysis Diagram

Matrix data analysis is a multivariate analysis technique called **"Principal Component Analysis"**. This technique quantifies and arranges data presented in a matrix diagram, to find more general indicators that differentiate and give clarity to large amount of complex, intertwined information. This can help us visualize properly and get an insight into situations.

This diagram is used when the matrix chart does not provide detailed information sufficiently. This is the only method within the New Seven Tools that is based on data analysis and gives numerical results.

Characteristics of Matrix Data Analysis Diagram

(*a*) The matrix analysis method qualifies and arranges matrix diagram data so that the information is easy to visualise and comprehend.

(*b*) The relationships between the elements shown in a matrix diagram are quantified by obtaining numerical data for intersection cells.

(*c*) Of the seven new QC tools, this is the only numerical analysis method. The results of this technique, however, are presented in the form of a diagram.

(*d*) One major technique that this method also utilises is known as the principal-component analysis.

Uses of Matrix Data Analysis Diagram

- Analyses production processes where factors are complexly intertwined.
- Analyses causes of non-conformities that involve a large volume of data.
- Graphs the desired quality levels indicated by the results of a market survey.
- Classifies sensory characteristics systematically.
- Accomplishes complex quality evaluations.
- Analyses curvilinear data.

3.10.6 Process Decision Programme Chart (PDPC)

The Process Decision Programme Chart (PDPC) is a very useful and powerful method to overcome an unfamiliar problem or a goal. With the help of PDPC we can map out all the conceivable events or contingencies that can occur in the implementation stage and also find feasible counter-measures to overcome these.

Characteristics of a PDPC

(*a*) The PDPC diagram is a simple graphical tool, which can be used to mitigate risk in virtually any undertaking.

(*b*) The PDPC method helps determine which processes to use to obtain desired results by evaluating the progress of events and the variety of conceivable outcomes.

(*c*) Implementation plans do not always progress as anticipated. When problems, technical or otherwise, arise, solutions are frequently not apparent.

(*d*) The PDPC method anticipates possible outcomes to such problems and prepares counter-measures that lead to the best possible solutions.

(*e*) Establishes an implementation plan for management by objectives.

(*f*) Establishes an implementation plan for technology-development themes.

(*g*) Establishes a policy of forecasting and responding in advance to major events predicted in the system.

(*h*) Implements counter-measures to minimise non-conformities in the manufacturing process to set up and select adjustment measures for a negotiating process.

Steps in Constructing a PDPC Chart

- Select a team that is familiar with the process and possible contingencies. Typically, this will be a group that 'knows' the effort or has made a similar effort earlier.
- Determine the flow of the plan activities and place them on a flow-chart or sequence.
- Construct a tree diagram, placing pre-requisite activities in a time sequence. This can be done in either a horizontal or vertical format.
- At each step, ask, "What can go wrong here" and place contingency on the chart.

- Determine plausible explanations/solutions to each problem identified above and place the solution on the chart.

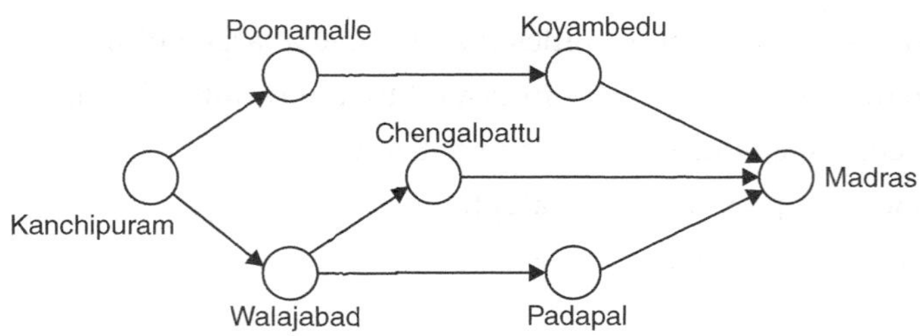

FIGURE 3.11 **Process Decision Programme Chart**

The above diagram shows that, Process decision programme charts help the user select the best processes to be used to accomplish a task. While the method has many variations, it basically lists out all the possible tasks in a process and task sequences of all the alternatives. The figure shows starting at some point and proceeding towards a goal. Each circle (node) is a separate task. In this figure, three different pathways are possible from start to end. The fundamental idea is that the goal can be reached in various ways however, only one of the sequences of tasks will be optimal. The PDPC assists in visualising the alternatives when planning a sequence of tasks in a process. Two major alternatives for analysing PDPCs are/used for forward planning and backward planning. Both are illustrated in the figure above. The method in forward planning is to begin at the start node and work towards the goal node by selecting the best path. In contrast, backward planning starts at the end node and moves towards the start.

3.10.7 Arrow Diagram

Arrow Diagram or Activity Network Diagram or Project Evaluation and Review Technique (PERT) or Critical Path Method (CPM). It uses a network representation to show the steps necessary to implement a plan. It is a network technique using nodes for events and arrows for activities for project planning, scheduling and monitoring. This is a very useful tool when we want to plan the activities of a known but complex task or project. With the help of this tool we can work out an ideal project plan and also a daily plan for not only the main task but also for other allied tasks and monitor their progress in an effective manner.

Steps in Constructing an Arrow Diagram

(*a*) Select a team that is knowledgeable about the project, its tasks and sub-tasks.

(*b*) Record all the tasks and sub-tasks necessary to the completion of the project.

(*c*) Sequence the tasks.

(*d*) Assign time duration to each task.

(*e*) Calculate the shortest possible implementation time schedule using the critical path method.

(*f*) Calculate the earliest starting and finishing times for each task.

(*g*) Locate tasks with slack (extra) time and calculate total slack.

(*h*) Update the schedule as the project is being completed.

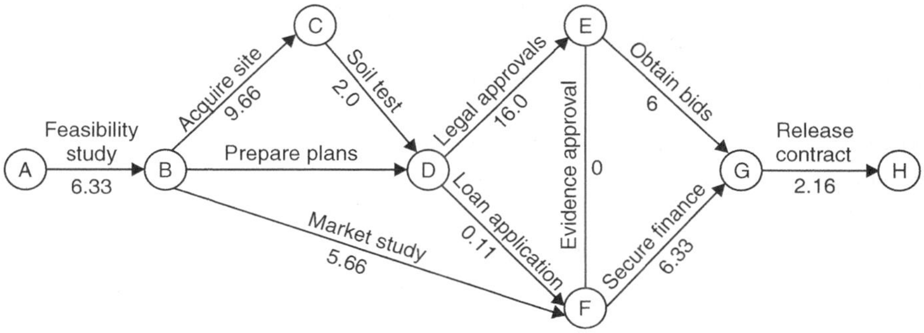

FIGURE 3.12 **Arrow Diagram**

Arrow diagrams display information about the operation of a process by using arrows and nodes. Arrow diagrams can be thought of as a way to understand the operation of a process using time, cost or other metrics.

Uses of Arrow Diagram

- It helps to understand and manage a complex project or task.
- It helps to understand and manage a project that is of major importance to the organisation and where the consequences of late completion are severe.
- It enables understanding and managing a project in which multiple activities must take place and be managed simultaneously.
- It enables explaining the project status to others.
- It helps to implement plans for new product development and its follow-up.
- It helps to develop product-improvement plans and follow-up activities.
- It helps to establish daily plans for experimental trials and follow-up activities.
- It helps to establish daily plans for increases in production and their follow-up activities.
- It helps to synchronies the preceding plans for QC activities.
- It helps to develop plans for a facility move and for monitoring follow-up.
- It helps to implement a periodic facility maintenance plan and it's follow-up.
- It helps to analyse a manufacturing process and draw up plans for improved efficiency.
- It helps to plan and follow-up QC inspections and diagnostic tests.
- It helps to plan and follow-up QC conferences and QC circle conferences.

3.10.8 Need for New Seven Tools and Their Benefits

There may be management situations where not all data needed for problem-solving is readily available. Much of problem-solving in management calls for collaboration among people from different departments. Here too, hard data is scarce, and that which is available is likely to be highly subjective. In such cases, it is necessary to go beyond the analytical approach and use the design approach for solving problems. The New Seven Tools used under this design approach have proved useful in areas such as product quality improvement, cost reduction, new-product development and policy deployment. The New Seven Tools are among the most effective for today's managers, staff and engineers.

The New Seven Tools are very useful for top and middle managements for strategic planning, goal Setting and problem solving. But these tools are not a replacement to the old seven tools. The knowledge of these basic seven tools is a must for every one-from the top management to the employee at the grassroots.

Unit 4

TQM Tools

4.1 BENCHMARKING

4.1.1 Introduction to Benchmarking

The Change is the only thing that does not change in the world. Benchmarking is a systematic method which is effectively used to

- Establish that there is a need for change.
- Entity what should be changed.
- Create a picture of how the organization should look after the change.

The people used the benchmarking without knowing what it is say for example.

- A former compares himself with another who gets much more yield and he practices that for his performance.
- A worker follows his fellow worker's practices for improving his performance.
- Student learns from his best in class and set his goal to achieve and to further claim up.
- A faculty changes his method of teaching by adopting the best practices from.
- His seniors or colleagues to make the learning more efficient.
- A government compares the standard of living of their people with another country and tries to implement practices for improving it.

And hence the purpose of benchmarking is to gain competitive advantage. The companies have started looking for new tools meet the changes brought by liberalization, privatization and globalization. They started the benchmarking for the purpose of comparing unit manufacturing costs to improve the quality. The companies realized that nothing much will happen by simply comparing the costs, prices and wage rates of employees. In 1983 Xerox Corporation implemented the benchmarking and it was found to be very successful. Later the companies Ford GTE, AT & T, DuPont, HP, IBM have started using benchmarking for improving their competitiveness.

4.1.2 Definition of Benchmarking

"The continuous process of measuring products, services and practices against the company's toughest competitors or those companies renowned as industry leaders".

—Camp

"Benchmarking is measuring performance against that of best-in-class organizations, determining how the best in class achieve those performance levels, and using the information as the basis for goals, strategies and implementation".

—Pryor

Both the definitions discuss two important issues namely measuring performance and why that differs from the competitors. Companies measure their performance and compare them with their competitor's performance. Then the company changes the process by setting goals, strategies and implementation.

4.1.3 Major Reasons to Benchmark

Globalization is one of the major reason that why the companies have to benchmark. Any company from any part of the world could be a competitor. Since the market is no longer protected. Hence, companies within in a nation need to imitate and assimilate the processes for the success of their business even within the nation if they are not interested to move out of the nation.

Benchmarking is an external orientation. Normally, the companies set their goals and objectives from the just previous year's experience and performance. They may not serve the purpose in the changed competition. Benchmarking allows the goals to be set objectively based on external information. The information shall be obtained from the followings:

- Site visits
- Reverse engineering
- Competitive analysis

The time and cost could be saved because the benchmarking partners provide a working model of an improved process which reduces some of the planning, testing and prototyping effort. The benchmarking process improves the commitment to continuous improvement. The actual benchmarking is done by process owners who know it best and most qualified to analyze it. They automatically develop a commitment to the process and resulting best practices.

The process owners will always look for potentially useful technological breakthroughs and try to adapt them at the earliest possible to be competitive in the marker.

4.1.4 Benchmarking Process

A benchmarking process shall consist of five major phases which may be broken into 12 steps. Planning, Analysis, Integration, Action and Maturity are the five phases:

Planning

- Decide what to benchmark.
- Decide whom to benchmark.
- Decide who should be on the benchmarking team.
- Determine the data collection method.
- Collect data.
- Investigate including the legal issues involved in benchmarking a competitor.
- Know what the some common pitfalls are.

Analysis

- Analyze the internal business processes and have full understanding of them. Choose the external business processes for comparing.
- Compare them and examine the competitive gap.
- Project the future performance levels.

Integration

- Communicate the benchmarking findings and get acceptance from the top management.
- Revise performance goals.
- Integrate the targets and strategies into business plans and functional goals.

Action

- Recalibrate the plans and have action plans.
- Implement the action plans Monitor the results and progress Recalibrate the benchmarks.

Maturity

- Determine whether you have become leader in the process.
- Continue to improve further.

STEP 1: What to Benchmark?

The company has to identify the customers and products. The bench marking project should focus on a task that is important for the company. Then Critical Success Factors (CSF) should be defined by concentrating on the product, customer and the company's mission. The Pareto analysis shall be used to prioritize the Critical Success Factors to select a benchmarking project. The success of a benchmarking project depends on selecting a worthwhile project.

STEP 2: Whom to Benchmark?

The Company should search for whom to benchmark to improve the performance. The company shall select a competitor's process which can produce breakthrough results. The benchmarking shall be classified as follows.

(*a*) Internal benchmarking
(*b*) Competitive benchmarking
(*c*) Functional benchmarking
- Process benchmarking
- Strategic benchmarking

(*d*) Partnering.

(*a*) **Internal benchmarking:** It is the comparison of practices among similar operations within a firm. Say for example a department may be performing an identical (or) similar work in an effective way and that may be benchmarked.

(*b*) **Competitive benchmarking:** It is the benchmarking done by choosing a competitor who is marked leader for the chosen benchmarking project. There need not be a direct benchmarking exchange with a competitor source such as professional associations, public seminars, lectures, trade shows and speeches before public audiences shall be used for collecting information. International Benchmarking clearing house had developed benchmarking code of contact to manage formal benchmarking.

(*c*) **Functional benchmarking:** Say, a company wants to improve its logistic operations by benchmarking. The company deals with wide varieties of products that had to be stored and shipped to the customers. The company shall think of benchmarking the function with that of best practices performed by Hospital equipments supplying company, couriers services company, departmental stores company and Tiffin box distributing firm and Mumbai city. Hence a company's best practicing function could be imitated and assimilated for continuously improving the performance of the company. It need not be from a competitor always. The functional benchmarking may be used for improving process improvement *i.e.,* process benchmarking or to establish a new strategy *i.e.,* strategic benchmarking.

(*d*) **Partnering:** The organization with which one would benchmark is known as a 'partner'. The success of partnering depends on the mutual benefits for both the organization via benchmarking.

STEP 3: Determine Data-Collection Method

Once the benchmarking team is formed, they shall find the ways and means of collecting data for improving the performance. The sources may be classified as follows:

- Internal
- External
- Original.

(*a*) **Internal:** Public libraries, company libraries and on-line libraries are some of the internal sources. Now-a-days on line searches are found to be useful due to the advent of internet.

(*b*) **External:** Conference, public seminars, professional associations, News letters, Journal, trade shows and lectures are some of the sources of external nature.

(*c*) **Original:** The benchmarking team can directly contact the potential companies through phone or mail. With a simple questionnaire. The team can shortlist the company's interested based on this first survey and detailed information shall be obtained through a questionnaire.

STEP 4: Collection of Data

The team should decide the kind of data which they need for their benchmarking activity. Say for example the following checklist may be followed in case the team wants to collect data by visiting the site.

- Plan the time and date of site visit.
- Prepare an agent for the site visit and exchange.
- Prepare the questions to be asked and send them to the benchmarking partners.
- Keep the team as much as possible small. *i.e.,* four members.
- Identify the individual areas of interest of the team and be ready to interact with the partners.
- All the data obtained shall be recorded instantly by a member (or) as soon as the meeting is over.
- Plan for review meetings.
- Prepare a site visit report.

STEP 5: Analyze the Performance Gap

The benchmarking team must analyze and identify gaps or differences that exist between the team's process and that of the best-in-class and that of world-class organization.

STEP 6: Project Performance Levels

The benchmarking team must keep in mind that the best-in-class company also planning improvement and hence the performance levels should be fixed high considering this point. The team should answer the questions such as given below by asking themselves.

- What is the current performance gap?
- How will industry performance change?
- Will the performance gap widen, narrow or remain the same?
- What are the implications for the subject business?
- How can the organization gain a significant performance advantage?

STEP 7: Communicate Findings

The team is responsible for communicating the findings to the top management and gets their approval for taking forward the project. The team should organize and present the findings recommendations to the people whom should they communicate.

STEP 8: Establish Functional Goals

On the acceptance of findings and recommendations, the team should identify the individuals who will be affected by the change and communicate to them the benefits. The goals and objectives of the departments concerned must be revised.

STEP 9: Develop Action Plans

The team must set priorities by developing an action plan and they should implement them after getting approval. The team should completes the following:

- Describe the specific tasks that must be completed and the results expected.
- Sequence the tasks chronologically and designate a targeted completion date for each.
- Assess the resources required to implement the best practices. This covers items such as budget, people, equipment and materials.
- Assigns responsibilities to specific, named individuals for each action item. Explain how to complete the task.
- Establish a monitoring system to track progress and alert the team when corrective action is required.

STEP 10: Implement Plan and Monitor Results

The benchmarking team should first implement simple project and show them the effects on performance improvements. Then the wholesale implementation of action plan must be begun. The team needs to establish measurements to gauge implementation progress using quality tools.

STEP 11: Recalibrate Benchmarks

The benchmarking team shall recalibrate the benchmarks based on the targets achieved. Recalibration is performed by exercising the previous steps.

STEP 12: Maturity

The maturity state comes only when the team becomes a leader in the process by making it efficient while it delights the customer. The cycle will be repeated for further improvements.

4.2 QUALITY FUNCTION DEPLOYMENT [QFD]

4.2.1 Introduction

The QFD methodology was first developed in Japan by Dr. Shigorce Mizuno in 1960's. But them this was popularly known as quality tables. The first application of QFD was at Mitsubishi, Heavy Industries Ltd., in the kobe shipyard, Japan in 1972, later, this was used by Toyota in the production of mini-vans. The QFD was introduced to United States by Dr. Clausing of Xerox in 1984. Since then the QFD has become one of the most important tool in Quality Planning Process.

A number of companies have implemented TQM but few have only reaped its full benefits. There are different approaches as performed by Juran, Crosby, Deming and Feigenbaum. Seven QC tools and Seven new QC tools are employed for implementing TQM. The TQM philosophy emphasizes the role of people, usually in multifunctional teams to bring about improvement from within the organization. The heart of the philosophy is the prevention of problem and an emphasis on quality in design and development of product and process. The QFD is one of the techniques which is a successful tool in quality planning process.

4.2.2 Quality Function Deployment

The products and services are developed quickly and inexpensively without sacrificing quality or losing focus of customer requirements. The QFD is found to be a tool due to the following reasons.

The QFD will save development time, which will reduce the costs and allow the company to respond more easily to changes in the market. The QFD will focus the company's resources on providing those capabilities that drive customer satisfaction. The QFD ensures that issued critical to the success of the product do not get dropped.

4.2.3 Definition of QFD

American Supplier Institute defined the QFD as "a system for translating customer requirements into appropriate company requirements at every stage, from research, through product design and development, to manufacture, distribution, installation and marketing, sales and service".

QFD is a team based management tool which ingrains the views of the customer into the products in a systematic involving all the departments/sections of manufacturing/service. Normally, the views of customers are popularly called as voice of the customers. *i.e.,* the customer requirements have to be referred in their terms of reference.

The voice of the customers can be collected from market survey and research. In the Phase I of QFD, the voice of the customers will form part of rows in a matrix structure while the part features will be in the columns. Phase II of QFD deals with part features Vs part characteristics. Phase III will deal with part characteristics Vs process characteristics. Phase IV will deal with process characteristics Vs control parameters.

4.2.4 Structure of QFD

The QFD chart looks like a house The left hand side of the chart is used to list what the customer expects in a product and hence this section is referred as "WHATS SECTION". The right hand of the chart is used to show importance rating, target value (or) goal, Improvement ratio (or) scale up factor, sales point and customer benchmarking etc. The left and right of the chart look like a left and right of a house. The top side of chart is used to list the Technical requirements or voice of the Engineers to meet the customer requirement. Each row *i.e.,* Customer requirements may be related one or more technical requirements (each column). The body of the chart is to show the relationship between Customer Requirements (CR) and Technical Requirements (TR). The technical requirements are known as "HOWS" to achieve the "WHATS". And the body looks like a interior of a House.

The top triangular part of the chart is used to show the interrelationship of the technical requirements and it looks like the roof the house. The bottom part of QFD chart is to represent technical competitiveness, targets and benchmarking etc. The bottom of the chart looks like a foundation of the house. And hence the QFD chart is very popularly known as House of Quality (HOQ) charts. The others QFD charts can make deploys columns of the current chart into rows of the next chart and find new "HOWS" to achieve the customer requirements taking them to various phases of manufacturing. The relationship between "WHATS" and "HOWS" are normally classified as weak, moderate and strong and they are rated numerically 1,3 and 9 respectively. They can also be represented symbolically as follows.

Example

A simple case is that how pencils quality shall be analyzed with QFD. A market research has to be conducted, identifying the voice of customers with importance rating (1 to 5 scales or 1 to 9 scales)

They may be as follows with their importance rating:

Importance rating

1. Easy to hold 3
2. Does not smear 5
3. Point lasts long 5
4. Does not roll 1

Solution

The voice of engineers shall be collected by giving them the outcome of market research. They provide the technical requirement to meet the above customer requirements. And they listed as follows.

- Length of pencil
- Time between sharpening
- Lead dust generated
- Hexagonally
- Minimum erasure residue.

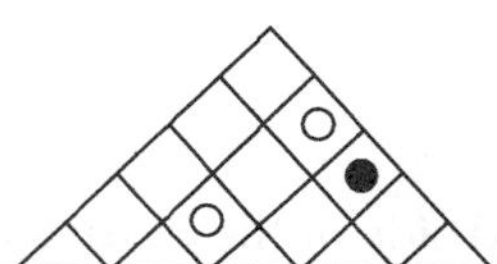

Customer requirements / Technical requirements	Importance	Length of pencil	Time between sharpening	Lead dust generated	Hexgonality	Minimal erasure residue	Goal	Improvement ratio	Sales point	Demanded weight	Relative weight	0 1 2 3 4 5
Easy to hold	3	●			●		3	0.6	1.0	1.8	7.4	
Does not smear	5		○	●		●	5	1.12	1.0	5.6	23.1	
Point lasts long	5	△	○	○		○	5	2.0	1.5	15	62.0	
Does not roll	1				●		3	0.6	1.0	1.8	7.4	
Absolute importance		99	255	302	74	302	1032					
Relative importance		9.6	24.7	29.3	7.2	29.3	100					

FIGURE 4.1 **QFD of Pencil**

A matrix is drawn as shown in the figure, using the voice of the customer and voice of the engineer. A brainstorming session shall be conducted to know the relationship between customer requirements and technical requirements. In this example, easy to hold is found to be strong with length of pencil and it is marked with the symbol. Similarly the relationships are filled for every other cell. The empty cell means that there is no relationship. The right hand side of the chart contains goal, improvement ratio, sales point, demanded weight and relative weight. Goal with 5 points means that the company wants to fix high the respective customer requirements. In this case "does not smear" and "point lasts" are considered with "5" point goal. While the other two are with 3 point goal. Improvement ration = Goal/Average of each row say, the improvement ratio for point lasts = 5/(3 + 5 + 5/3) = 5/4.3.

Likewise, the other rows are filled. The sales point is the customer requirement with which the company wants to sell the product. Normally 1.5, 1.2 and 1.0 are the points given for a customer requirement. The point lasts is given a 1.5 point in this case while the others are at 1.0. The demanded weights is the product of goal, improvement ratio and sales point. The Customer requirements with the higher relative weights are normally focused for improving the quality of the pencil. The column with average gives the absolute importance. The relative importance of technical requirements is the sum of the product of relative weight and cell relationship values. The technical requirements are sincerely attended by the company for which the relative importance is high. The right hand side of the chart *i.e.,* graph shows the present competitive level of the product. A competitor can be compared for each customer requirement and benchmarked for improvement.

The roof top of the chart represents the co-relationship between the technical requirements. In this case time between sharpening has a positive co-relation with lead dust generated and minimal erasure residue. When we involve only one chart to do the quality improvement, shall designate the chart as House of Quality Chart. When we go in for move than one deployment chart, then the charts shall be called as Quality Function Deployment Charts.

The customer requirements timely delivery, graphite size, free from dimensional deviation and good surface finish are the areas in which the improvements are expected. They are indicated by higher demanded weights as it is shown in figure. The functional weights indicates that the design of pattern and construction, schedule as per order and sand preparation are the control parameters need to be attended for improvement of quality while they continue to maintain the other parameters.

4.3 TAGUCHI'S QUALITY LOSS FUNCTION

4.3.1 Introduction

There are various measures used to measure the quality level. Percentage defectives, process capability index and warranty cost are some of the measures of quality level of shipped products. The percent defectives (or) warranty costs are understandable quality measures by anybody because they are related or converted cost. However, the customers are put to hardships due to time lag in taking action against warranty claims. On the other hand, the process capability indexes are used to measure quality but not as a cost problem. The actual significance of process capability index changes from a particular value to another value cannot be equally understood.

4.3.2 Uses of the Loss Function

The total loss due to the deviation of the product from its target value can be calculated. It can be used to compare the current process and improved process.

4.3.3 Loss Function and Types of Tolerances

Normally three different types of tolerances are employed in production/service. They are normally

- The Nominal—The Best (N-type),
- The Smaller—The Better (S-type),
- The Larger—The Better (L-type)

(*a*) **The Nominal—The Best (N-type):** Bilateral tolerances are used in this type of tolerance system. Under N-type, the tolerance is related to a basic dimension and is given in two directions in plus and minus.

(*b*) **The Smaller—The Better (S-type):** The specification of certain quality characteristics such as wear, shrinkage, noise level and impurity etc will be zero or positive but not negative. In this type, the quality characteristics will be greater than or equal to zero. *i.e.*, Y • 0 and the target value 'm' is zero. Therefore the loss function can be written as L(Y) = A (Y-m)2

4.4 TOTAL PRODUCTIVE MAINTENANCE

Good maintenance is fundamental to a productive manufacturing system; try running a production line with faulty equipment. Total Productive Maintenance (TPM) is keeping the current plant and equipment at its highest productive level through cooperation of all areas of the organization. Generally, the first bridge to cross is to breakdown the traditional barriers between maintenance and production personnel so they are working together. Individuals working together without regard to organizational structure, using their skills and ingenuity, have a common objective-peak performance or total productivity.

This approach does not mean that such basic techniques as predictive and preventative maintenance are not used; they are essential to building a foundation for a successful TPM environment. Predictive maintenance is the process of using data and statistical tools to determine when a piece of equipment will fail, and preventative maintenance is the process of periodically performing activities such as lubrication on the equipment to keep it running.

The total maintenance function should be directed towards the elimination of un-planned equipment and plant maintenance. The objective is to create a system in which all maintenance activities can be planned and not interfere with the production process. Surprise equipment breakdowns should not occur. Before the advent of computer-aided manufacturing, operators in some organizations were responsible for their machines and took a certain pride of ownership. With the help of maintenance technicians, operators spent part of their work time keeping their equipment in good running order. Recent technical advances have given us more tools to perform the maintenance function.

Analyzing TPM into its three words, we have:

Total = All encompassing by maintenance and production individuals working together.

Productive = Production of goods and services that meet or exceed customers expectations.

Maintenance = Keeping equipment and plant in as good as or better than the original condition at all times.

4.4.1 Objectives of TPM

- Maintaining and improving equipment capacity.
- Maintaining equipment for life.
- Using support from all areas of the operation.
- Encouraging input from all employees.
- Using teams for continuous improvement.

4.4.2 Steps in TPM

The first activity in any assessment of performance is to determine the current operating parameters. Where are we today? What systems do we have in place, and how do they work? What is the current condition of the plant and equipment? Are we starting from scratch, or do we have workable systems that only need to be improved? Total Productive Maintenance (TPM) is an extension of the Total Quality Management (TQM) philosophy to the maintenance function. Seven basic steps get an organization started toward TPM:

- Management learns the new philosophy.
- Management promotes the new philosophy.
- Training is funded and developed for everyone in the organization.
- Areas of needed improvement are identified.
- Performance goals are formulated.
- An implementation plan is developed.
- Autonomous work groups are established.

There is no single correct method for implementation; however, these steps will provide a good framework.

(*a*) **Learn the New Philosophy:** One of the most difficult things for senior management to deal with change. They need to learn about TPM and how it will affect their operations. There are many successful examples; there are also many organizations that have tried various techniques to improve performance and failed. Benchmarking with a successful organization will provide valuable information. Any cultural change takes a special dedication to long-term improvement. The easy approach is to accept today's good performance numbers and say, "Why change?" Unfortunately your competitors are most likely improving and will be far ahead of you in the future. There also exists, in management, the concept that somehow because "I am the chief, I know more than those who work here." TPM is merely trying to tap into an unused resource, the brain power and problem-solving ability of all the organization's employees. Thus, it is necessary to allow people to make decisions. This approach is not permissive management, because management is still responsible for the performance of the organization. It does, however, represent a different way of managing.

Many organizations have had the flavor-of-the-month approach to changing management techniques. This approach has led to credibility problems with employees. Management is changed and the new person does not build on past accomplishments but comes a "new system" that will presumably solve all of the organization's problems. Lack of ownership seems to cause low morale and dissatisfaction with management. Ownership should be based on what is good for the customer and for the employees that serve the customer. A look at approaches at Southwest Airlines or Hewlett Packard helps to understand what needs to be done. These organizations, and others, emphasize employee well-being and empowerment. It is difficult to argue with their performance numbers. Initially this change will require more work by management. Eventually, it will mean less work as all individuals start solving their own problems.

(*b*) **Promoting the Philosophy:** Senior management must spend significant time in promoting the system. They must sell the idea and let the employees know that they are totally committed to its success.Like TQM or any other major change in an organization, there must be total commitment from the top. If the belief in the new philosophy and commitment are not there, then positive results will not happen. Too often lip service is given to a "new idea." This action is usually brought on by a belief that the new system will solve some immediate problems and lead to an immediate return on investment. A long-term commitment to the new philosophy is required. It has been proven by other organizations to be a better way of doing business.

Management should lead the way by practicing the new philosophy. Organizations that are having difficulties owe it, in part, to insincere leadership. One of the best ways to implement the new philosophy is just to start doing it. In other words, start giving the maintenance and production personnel more autonomy. Once the employees realize that management is serious about taking the organization in a new, more positive direction, employees usually respond. Introducing TPM with a huge fanfare leads employees to shrug it off as the latest method for getting them to work harder. Management must first build credibility, and the best way to accomplish that task is to change first and lead the way.

(*c*) **Training:** Teach the philosophy to managers at all levels. Begin with senior management, and work down to first-line supervisors. Senior management must spend time learning about and understanding the ratifications of applying this philosophy to their organization. Is senior management dedicated to the long-term commitment required to achieve positive results? Some managers may need to be replaced or take early retirement because they will not change their way of dealing with people. Those managers who readily respond to the new philosophy should also be identified. Middle management must learn how to deal with the team approach and how small autonomous work groups function. This organizational level seems to have the greatest difficulty with this type of change. In recent years, downsizing has come at the expense of middle managers. Of course, historically this has been an inflated area of management. The philosophies that are promoted within TPM and TQM management structures. When you allow people to make their own decisions you do not need as many lawyers of managers making sure employers are doing their job correctly. First-line supervisors need to learn their role in what most likely will be a new environment. Supervisors who have been used to guiding their groups will find this an easy transition. Those managers who have been telling employees everything to do will find this difficult. Supervisors will relinquish some of their power, although that power may be more perceived than actual. The day of the autocratic manager has disappeared. A highly educated workforce does not tolerate that management style. In reality, a supervisor is only as good as their ability to coach their team. Employees need to learn about the various tools used in performing their tasks as part of an autonomous work group.There needs to be some instruction in the area of jobs that maintenance people do and jobs that production people do. A great benefit of TPM is the cross-pollination of ideas between maintenance technicians and production operators.

(*d*) **Improvement Needs:** There are usually some machines that seem to be on the verge of breaking down or require an excessive amount of maintenance. Employees who work with the equipment on a daily basis are better able to identify these conditions than anyone else in the Organization. A good first step is to let the operators and maintenance technicians tell management which machines and systems need the most attention. An implementation team of operators and technicians to coordinate this process is essential. This action will build credibility and start the organization towards TPM. One of the first steps for the team is to identify the current status. In other words, what is the baseline?

The following measurements were developed by the Japanese and are accepted by most practitioners. Six major loss areas need to be measured and tracked:

(*i*) **Downtime losses**

- **Planned**
  - Start-ups
  - Shift changes
  - Coffee and lunch-breaks
  - Planned maintenance shutdowns
- **Unplanned Downtime**
  - Equipment breakdown
  - Changeovers
  - Lack of material
  - Reduced speed losses
- **Idling and minor stoppages**
- **Slow-downs**

(*ii*) **Poor quality losses**

- *Process* nonconformities
- Scrap

These losses can be quantified into three metrics and can be summarized into one equipment effectiveness metric. Equations for these metrics follow.

Downtime losses are measured by equipment availability using the equation

$$A = (T/P) \times 100$$

where A = availability

T = operating time ($P - D$)

P = planned operating time

D = downtime

Reduced speed losses are measured by tracking performance efficiency using the equation

$$E = (C \times N/T) \times 100$$

where, E = performance efficiency

C = theoretical cycle time

N = processed amount (quantity)

Poor quality losses are measured by tracking the rate of quality products produced using the equation

$$R = (N - Q) \times 100$$

where, R = rate of quality products

N = Processes amount (quantity)

Q = nonconformities

Equipment effectiveness is measured as the product of the decimal equivalent of the three previous metrics using the equation

$$EE = A * E * R$$

where EE = equipment effectiveness, or overall equipment effectiveness (OEE) The target for improvement is 85% equipment effectiveness.

(*e*) **Goal:** Goals should be set after the improvement needs are identified. A good first goal is to establish the timeframe for fixing the first prioritized problem. Technicians and operators will probably want it done faster than management because it causes them more problems on a daily basis. Identifying needs and setting goals begins the process of getting the organization to work together as a team.

(*f*) **Developing Plans:** First develop and implement an overall plan of action for training all employees. Plans for developing the autonomous work groups should take place during the training phase. Plan to use teams of maintenance technicians and operators to work on particularly troublesome problems. Priorities can be set and management can make a commitment with resources to correct some of the basic problems. Using the team approach will set the stage for the development of autonomous work groups, which are teams established for daily operations. At this point, employees should have input into how these autonomous teams are structured. Part of the planning process should take into consideration that autonomous work groups will change over time. As processes and procedures are improved, the structure of the whole organization will change. It would be unreasonable not to expect autonomous work groups to change also.

(*g*) **Autonomous Work Groups:** Autonomous work groups are established based on the natural flow of activity. First, make the operator responsible for the equipment and the level of maintenance that he is capable of performing. Next, identify the maintenance personnel who work in certain areas or have certain skill levels. Operators and maintenance personnel are brought together, resulting in an autonomous work group. These groups must have the authority to make decisions about keeping the equipment in first-class running order.

4.5 FAILURE MODES AND EFFECTS ANALYSIS [FMEA] INTRODUCTION

Customers are placing increased demands on companies for high quality, reliable products. The increasing capabilities and functionality of many products are making it more difficult for manufacturers to maintain the quality and reliability. Traditionally, reliability has been achieved through extensive testing and use of techniques such as probabilistic reliability modeling. These are techniques done in the late stages of development. The challenge is to design in quality and reliability early in the development cycle.

Failure Modes and Effects Analysis (FMEA) is methodology for analyzing potential reliability problems early in the development cycle where it is easier to take actions to overcome these issues, thereby enhancing reliability through design. FMEA is used to identify potential failure modes, determine their effect on the operation of the product, and identify actions to mitigate the failures. A crucial step is anticipating what might go wrong with a product. While anticipating every failure mode is not possible, the development team should formulate as extensive a list of potential failure modes as possible.

The early and consistent use of FMEAs in the design process allows the engineer to design out failures and produce reliable, safe, and customer pleasing products. FMEAs also capture historical information for use in future product improvement.

4.5.1 Types of FMEA's

There are several types of FMEAs, some are used much more often than others. FMEAs should always be done whenever failures would mean potential harm or injury to the user of the end item being designed. The types of FMEA are:

- System—focuses on global system functions
- Design—focuses on components and subsystems
- Process—focuses on manufacturing and assembly processes
- Service—focuses on service functions
- Software—focuses on software functions.

(*a*) **System FMEA:** This is used to analyze systems and subsystems in the early concept and design stage. A system FMEA focuses on potential failure modes between the functions of the system caused by system deficiencies. It includes the interactions between systems and elements of the system.

The outputs of the system FMEA are:

- A potential list of failure modes ranked by RPN.
- A potential list of system functions that could detect potential failure modes.
- A potential list of design actions to eliminate failure modes, safety issues and reduces the occurrence.

The benefits of the system FMEA are that it:

- Helps to select the optimum system alternative.
- Helps to determine redundancy.
- Helps to define the basis for system level diagnostic procedures.
- Increases the likelihood that potential problems will be considered.
- Identifies potential system failures and their interaction with other systems.

(*b*) **Design FMEA:** This is used to analyze products before they are released to manufacturing. A design focuses on failure modes caused by design deficiencies.

The outputs of the design FMEA are:

- A potential list of failure modes ranked by RPN.
- A potential list of critical and/or significant characteristics.
- A potential list of design actions to eliminate failure modes, safety issues and reduces the occurrence.
- A potential list of parameters for appropriate testing, inspection, and/or detection methods.
- A potential list of recommended action for the critical and significant characteristics.

The benefits of design FMEA are that it:

- Establishes a priority for design improvement actions.
- Documents the rationale for changes.
- Provides information to help through design verification and testing.
- Helps to identify the critical or significant characteristics.
- Assists in the evaluation of design requirements and alternatives.
- Helps to identify and eliminate potential safety concerns.
- Helps to identify product failure early in the product development phase.

(*c*) **Process FMEA:** This is used to analyze manufacturing and assembly processes. A process FMEA focuses on failure modes caused by process or assembly deficiencies.

The outputs of the process FMEA are: -

- A potential list of failure modes ranked by RPN.

- A potential list of critical and/ or significant characteristics.
- A potential list of recommended actions to address the critical and significant characteristics.
- A potential list to eliminate the causes of failure modes, reduce their occurrences, and improve defect detection if CPK cannot be improved.

The benefits of the process FMEA are that it: -

- Identifies process deficiencies and offers a corrective action plan.
- Identifies the critical and/ or significant characteristics and helps in developing control plans.
- Establishes a priority of corrective actions.
- Assists in the analysis of the manufacturing or assembly process.
- Documents the rationale for changes.

(*d*) **Service FMEA:** This is used to analyze services before they reach the customer. A service FMEA focuses on the failure modes (tasks, errors, mistakes) caused by system or process deficiencies.

The outputs of the service FMEA are:

- A potential list of errors ranked by RPN.
- A potential list of critical or significant tasks, or processes.
- A potential list of bottleneck processes or tasks.
- Potential list to eliminate the errors.
- A potential list of monitoring system/process functions.

The benefits of the service FMEA are that it:

- Assists in the analysis of job flow.
- Assists in the analysis of the system and/or process.
- Identifies task deficiencies.
- Identifies critical or significant tasks and helps in the development of control plan.
- Establishes a priority for improvement actions.
- Documents the rationale for changes.

4.5.2 Conditions of FMEA

- When new systems, designs, products, processes, or services are designed.
- When existing systems, designs, products, processes, or services are about to change regardless of reason.
- When new applications are found the existing conditions of the systems, designs, products, processes, or service.
- When improvements are considered for the existing systems, designs, products, processes, or services.

4.5.3 Purpose of FMEA

The purpose of performing an FMEA is to analyze the product's design characteristics relative to the planned manufacturing process and experiment design to ensure that the resultant product meets customer needs and expectations. When potential failure modes are identified, corrective action can be taken to eliminate them or to continually reduce a potential occurrence. The FMEA also documents the rationale for the chosen manufacturing process. It provides for an organized critical analysis of potential failure modes and the associated causes for the system being defined. The technique uses occurrence and detection probabilities in conjunction with a severity criteria to develop a risk priority number (RPN) for ranking corrective action considerations.

The FMEA can be performed as either a hardware or functional analysis. The hardware approach requires parts identification from engineering drawings (schematics, bill of materials) and reliability performance data, for example mean time between failures (MTBF), and is generally performed in a part-level fashion (bottom-up). However, it can be initiated at any level (component/assembly/subsystem) and progress in either direction (up or down).

Typically, the functional approach is used when hardware items have not been uniquely identified or when system complexity requires analysis from the system level downward (topdown). This normally occurs during the design development stages of the equipment life cycle; however, any subsystem FMEA can be performed at any time. Although FMEA analyses vary from hardware to software, and from components (*i.e.*, integrated circuits, bearings) to system (*i.e.*, stepper, furnace), the goal is always the same: to design reliability into the equipment.

Thus, a functional analysis to FMEA on a subassembly is appropriate to use as a case study for the purposes of this guideline.

4.5.4 Benefits of FMEA

FMEA is designed to assist the engineer improve the quality and reliability of design. Properly used the FMEA provides the engineer several benefits. Among others, these benefits include:

- Improve product/process reliability and quality.
- Increase customer satisfaction.
- Early identification and elimination of potential product/process failure modes.
- Prioritize product/process deficiencies.
- Capture engineering/organization knowledge.
- Emphasizes problem prevention.
- Documents risk and actions taken to reduce risk.
- Provide focus for improved testing and development.
- Minimizes late changes and associated cost.
- Catalyst for teamwork and idea exchange between functions.

4.5.5 Who Performs the FMEA?

The FMEA should be initiated by the design engineer for the hardware approach, and the systems engineer for the functional approach. Once the initial FMEA has been completed, the entire engineering team should participate in the review process. The team will review for consensus and identify the high-risk areas that must be addressed to ensure completeness. Changes are then identified and implemented for improved reliability of the product.

The following is a suggested team for conducting/reviewing an FMEA:

(*a*) Project Manager

(*b*) Design Engineer (hardware/software/systems)

(*c*) Test Engineer

(*d*) Reliability Engineer

(*e*) Quality Engineer

(*f*) Field Service Engineer

(*g*) Manufacturing/Process Engineer

(*h*) Safety Engineering

Outside supplier engineering and/or manufacturing could be added to the team. Customer representation is recommended if a joint development program between user/supplier exists.

4.5.6 Stages of FMEA (Process)

Since the FMEA concentrates on identifying possible failure modes and their effects on the equipment, design deficiencies can be identified and improvements can be made. Identification of potential failure modes leads to a recommendation for an effective reliability program. Priorities on the failure modes can be set according to the FMEA's risk priority number (RPN) system. A concentrated effort can be placed on the higher RPN items based on the Pareto analysis obtained from the analysis. As the equipment proceeds through the life cycle phases, the FMEA analysis becomes more detailed and should be continued. The FMEA process consists of the following stages

(*a*) FMEA prerequisites

(*b*) Functional block diagram

(*c*) Failure mode analysis and preparation of work sheets

(*d*) Team review

(*e*) Corrective action.

4.5.7 FMEA Procedure

The process for conducting an FMEA is straightforward. The basic steps are outlined below.

1. **Describe the product/process and its function:** An understanding of the product or process under consideration is important to have clearly articulated. This understanding simplifies the process of analysis by helping the engineer identify those product/process uses that fall within the intended function and which ones fall outside. It is important to consider both intentional and unintentional uses since product failure often ends in litigation, which can be costly and time consuming.

2. **Create a bock diagram of the product or process:** A block diagram of the product/process should be developed. This diagram shows major components or process steps as blocks connected together by lines that indicate how the components or steps are related. The diagram shows the logical relationships of components and establishes a structure around which the FMEA can be developed. Establish a Coding System to identify system elements. The block diagram should always be included with the FMEA form.
3. **Complete the header on the FMEA Form worksheet:** Product/System, Subsystem, Component, Design Lead, Prepared By, Date, Revision (letter or number), and Revision Date. Modify these headings as needed.
4. **Use the diagram prepared above to begin listing items or functions:** If items are components, list them in a logical manner under their subsystem/assembly based on the block diagram.
5. **Identify failure modes:** A failure mode is defined as the manner in which a component, subsystem, system, process, etc. could potentially fail to meet the design intent. Examples of potential failure modes include:
   - Corrosion
   - Hydrogen embitterment
   - Electrical Short or Open
   - Torque Fatigue
   - Deformation
   - Cracking.
6. **A failure mode in one component can serve as the cause of a failure mode in another component:** Each failure should be listed in technical terms. Failure modes should be listed for function of each component or process step. At this point the failure mode should be identified whether or not the failure is likely to occur. Looking at similar products or processes and the failures that have been documented for them is an excellent starting point.
7. **Describe the effects of those failure modes:** For each failure mode identified the engineer should determine what the ultimate effect will be. A failure effect is defined as the result of a failure mode on the function of the product/process as perceived by the customer. They should be described in terms of what the customer might see or experience should the identified failure mode occur. Keep in mind the internal as well as the external customer. Examples of failure effects include:
   - Injury to the user
   - Inoperability of the product or process
   - Improper appearance of the product or process
   - Odors
   - Degraded performance
   - Noise.

Establish a numerical ranking for the severity of the effect. A common industry standard scale uses 1 to represent no effect and 10 to indicate very severe with failure affecting system operation and safety without warning. The intent of the ranking is to help the analyst determine whether a failure would be a minor nuisance or a catastrophic occurrence to the customer. This enables the engineer to prioritize the failures and address the real big issues first.

8. **Identify the causes for each failure mode:** A failure cause is defined as a design weakness that may result in a failure. The potential causes for each failure mode should be identified and documented. The causes should be listed in technical terms and not in terms of symptoms. Examples of potential causes include:
   - Improper torque applied
   - Improper operating conditions
   - Contamination
   - Erroneous algorithms
   - Improper alignment
   - Excessive loading
   - Excessive voltage
9. **Enter the probability factor:** A numerical weight should be assigned to each cause that indicates how likely that cause is (probability of the cause occuring). A common industry standard scale uses 1 to represent not likely and 10 to indicate inevitable.
10. **Identify current controls (design or process):** Current Controls (design or process) are the mechanisms that prevent the cause of the failure mode from occurring or which detect the failure before it reaches the Customer. The engineer should now identify testing, analysis, monitoring, and other techniques that can or have been used on the same or similar products/processes to detect failures. Each of these controls should be assessed to determine how well it is expected to identify or detect failure modes. After a new product or process has been in use previously undetected or unidentified failure modes may appear. The FMEA should then be updated and plans made to address those failures to eliminate them from the product/process.
11. **Determine the likelihood of detection:** Detection is an assessment of the likelihood that the Current Controls (design and process) will detect the Cause of the Failure Mode or the Failure Mode itself, thus preventing it from reaching the Customer. Based on the Current Controls, consider the likelihood of detection using the following table for guidance.
12. **Review risk priority numbers (RPN):** The Risk Priority Number is a mathematical product of the numerical Severity, Probability, and Detection ratings:

    $$\text{RPN} = (\text{Severity}) \times (\text{Probability}) \times (\text{Detection})$$

    The RPN is used to prioritize items than require additional quality planning or action.
13. **Determine recommended action(s) to address potential failures that have a high RPN:** These actions could include specific inspection, testing or quality procedures; selection of different components or materials; de-rating; limiting environmental stresses or

operating range; redesign of the item to avoid the failure mode; monitoring mechanisms; performing preventative maintenance; and inclusion of back-up systems or redundancy.

14. **Assign responsibility and a target completion date for these actions:** This makes responsibility clear-cut and facilitates tracking.
15. **Indicate actions taken:** After these actions have been taken, re-assess the severity, probability and detection and review the revised RPN's. Are any further actions required?
16. **Update the FMEA** as the design or process changes, the assessment changes or new information becomes known.

Unit 5 QUALITY SYSTEMS

5.1 INTRODUCTION TO QUALITY SYSTEM

It is learnt that the essence of the number of 'quality' definitions is to provide company's operating systems which promote conformance to specifications. Also the ever-increasing pressure to provide better quality of products led to the adoption of the concept of quality systems.

5.2 DEFINITION OF QUALITY SYSTEM

International Organization for Standardization (ISO) defined the term quality system as "*The quality systems are the organizational structures, responsibilities, procedures, processes and resources for implementing quality management*".

The quality system should function in such a manner as to provide proper confidence that:

- The system is well understood and effective.
- The products or services actually do satisfy customer expectations.
- The emphasis is placed on problem-prevention rather than dependence on detection, after occurrence.

In short, a quality system involves:

- How—methods and process description
- Who—responsibilities and authorities
- When—records and evidence ; and
- Where—identification and traceability.

5.3 REASONS FOR IMPLEMENTING A QUALITY SYSTEM

Users' experience clearly indicates the several significant improvements in the following areas:

- Improved employee involvement (average gain is 100%).
- Improved housekeeping (average gain is 140%).
- Improved decision-making based on facts and data (average gain is 95%).
- Improved customer satisfaction (gain is 55%).
- Improved safe working (gain is 45%).
- Reduced customer complaints (about 40%).
- Reduced inspection efforts (about 45%).
- Reduced quality cost (about 50%).

Now, in order sustain in the global market, many organizations are feeling the pressure of producing products in conformance with an ISO standard.

5.4 INTRODUCTION TO ISO

The International Organisation for Standardisation (ISO) was established in 1946 in Geneva, Switzerland, where it is still based.

- ISO is an association of National Standards Bodies of more than 150 countries.
- ISO is a specialized agency for standardization. The primary objective of ISO is coordination and unification of international standards.
- ISO employs a system of technical committees, sub-committees and working groups to develop international standards. Besides the national standard bodies, ISO permits other international organizations that develop standards to participate in its work, by accepting them as Liaison members.
- ISO works in accordance with an agreed set of rules of procedures, the ISO directives, which also include requirements on the presentation of standards.
- The Bureau of Indian Standards (BIS) is the national standards body of India represented on ISO.

5.4.1 ISO 9000 and ISO 14000—In Brief

The majority of ISO standards are highly specific to a particular product, material, or process. However, both ISO 9000 and ISO 14000 are known as generic management standards.

ISO 9000 has become an international reference for quality management requirements in business-to-business dealings, and ISO 14000 is for environmental management requirements.

The ISO 9000 family is primarily concerned with "quality management". This means what the organization does to fulfill:

- the customer's quality requirements, and
- applicable regulatory requirements, while aiming to

- enhance customer satisfaction, and
- achieve continual improvement of its performance in pursuit of these objectives.

The ISO 14000 family is primarily concerned with "environmental management": This means what the organisation does to:

- minimise harmful effects on the environment caused by it activities, and
- to achieve continual improvement of its environmental performance.

Both ISO 9000 and ISO 14000 concern the way an organization goes about its work, and not directly the result of this work. In other words, they both concern processes, and not products.

5.4.2 Need for ISO 9000 and Other Quality Systems

Every organization is concerned with the quality of its product or service. To assure the quality one has to ensure the quality. To ensure the quality it is necessary to make quality assurance system. Sound quality assurance system requires well defined quality system standards.

Quality and standardization are the two essential pre-requisites for an organization to market its products and services in the competitive business environment. Thus quality begins with standards. Also the ever-increasing pressure to provide better quality of products/services led to the development of quality standards.

5.5 ISO 9000 QUALITY SYSTEM

5.5.1 Meaning of ISO 9000 Standards

The ISO 9000 standards are a collection of formal International Standards, technical reports, handbooks and web based documents on quality management and quality assurance.

5.5.2 Who is Responsible for Developing the ISO 9000 Standards ?

ISO technical committee and its sub-committees are responsible for the development of the standards. The work is conducted on the basis of "consensus" among quality and industry experts nominated by the national standards bodies, representing a wide range of interested parties.

5.5.3 ISO 9000 (Series of Standards)

The ISO 9000 series of standards are generic rather than industry specific. It can be applied to any organization, large or small, whether its product, and whether it is a business enterprise, a public administration, or a government department.

It is concerned with the set of activities undertaken by an organization to ensure that its output provides customer satisfaction. It does not specify methods or procedures for achieving customer satisfaction; instead it describes concepts and objectives for achieving it.

5.5.4 Classification of ISO 9000 Quality System Standards

Following are the classification of ISO 9000 Quality System Standards and corresponding Indian Stanards are given in paranthesis.

(*a*) **ISO 8402: 1986 (IS 13999: 1988)—Vocabulary:** The ISO 8402 series of standards gives the definitions of various terms (such as quality, inspection, reliability, grade, quality assurance, etc.) used in the development of standards on quality systems.

The definitions listed in this series are used for understanding the quality concepts, preparation of quality standards and to avoid ambiguity in understanding the terms related to quality.

(*b*) **ISO 9001: 1987 (IS 14001: 1988)—Models for Quality Assurance:** The ISO 9001 standard gives a model for quality assurance at all stages starting from designing the product and continuing even after the product is delivered to the customer.

ISO 9001 is to be used when conformance to specified requirements is to be assured during design, development, production, and installation and servicing.

ISO 9001 can be applied to industries who design, produce, install product and provide service after sales as per the requirements of the customer. Examples of such products are heat exchangers, coolers, filters, pumps, etc. for process industries.

(*c*) **ISO 9002: 1987 (IS 14002: 1988)—Model for Quality Assurance in Production and Installation :** ISO 9002 gives a model for quality assurance in production and installation.

ISO 9002 is to be used when conformance to specified requirements is to be assured during production and installation. ISO 9002 can be applied to some products which require quality assurance only during production and till they are delivered to the customer or installed in his / her premises. In simple words, this model is applicable where the assurance on quality is required only during production and upto satisfactory installation. Examples of such products are: civil structures, construction of bridge, etc.

(*d*) **ISO 9003: 1987 (IS 14003: 1988)—Model for Quality Assurance in Final Inspection and Test:** ISO 9003 standard gives a model for quality assurance in final inspection and test. ISO 9003 is to be used when conformance to specified requirements is to be assured only at final inspection and testing. ISO 9003 can be applied to certain products which require quality assurance only after they are manufactured *i.e.*, quality assurance is required only in final inspection and test. For example, almost all the consumer items fall in this category. Some of the products are: domestic appliances, petroleum products, automobile components, etc.

(*e*) **ISO 9004: 1987 (IS 14004: 1991)—Quality Management and Quality System Elements Guidelines:** ISO 9004 gives guidelines for quality management in non-contractual situations.

ISO 9001, 9002 and 9003 are applied where a contract between supplier and contractor exists. In non-contractual situations, industries can apply ISO 9004 for quality management guidelines. In order to build confidence of the customer and to maintain quality culture in the organization, ISO 9004 gives guidelines comprising different elements of a quality management system.

(*f*) **ISO 10011-1: 1990 to 10011-3: 1990 (IS 14011 Part 1: 1990 to IS 14011 Part 3:1990)—Guidelines for Auditing Quality Systems:** This series deals with quality system auditing. It consists of three parts as given below:

- ISO 10011-1 describes the rule of auditors, their responsibilities, the elements of auditing, executing the audit, reporting, etc.
- ISO 10011-2 deals with the qualification criteria for quality system auditors; their capabilities to perform the audit and their freedom from influence. It also gives guidelines for evaluating auditor candidates.
- ISO 10011-3 deals with establishment of audit function.

5.5.5 Comparison between ISO 9001, 9002 and 9003

The following table provides a comparison of the parts of the various standards.

ISO 9001	ISO 9002	ISO 9003
Design	—	—
Manufacture	Manufacture	—
Test	Test	Test

It can be seen that all the requirements of ISO 9003 are included in ISO 9002 and all the requirements of ISO 9002 and ISO 9003 are included in ISO 9001. The sections in each part of the standards are the same. Therefore, the main differences between the ISO 9001, 9002 and 9003 are related to only the presence or absence of certain sections of the standards.

5.5.6 ISO 9001 Vs ISO 9004

ISO 9001 can be used for internal application by organisations for certification or contractual purposes.

ISO 9004 is not intended for certification or contractual purposes. It is used in no contractual situations.

ISO 9004 gives guidance on wider range of objectives of a quality management system than ISO 9001, with respect to organisation's continuous improvement and performance.

5.5.7 Elements (or) Clauses of ISO 9000 (or) Quality System Requirements

The elements of ISO 9000 must be understood for their successful implementation in an organization. The following are the twenty elements of a quality system:

(*i*) **Management Responsibility**

- The management should define and document its quality policy and objectives.
- The responsibility, authority and interrelations of all the employees should be clearly defined.
- The management should provide adequate resources for internal verification activities.

- The management should nominate management representative such as quality director or quality manager to coordinate the quality activity.
- The management must periodically review the effectiveness of the quality system and keep record of the same.

(*ii*) **Quality System**

- The organisation should document, establish and maintain a quality system.
- The documentation of quality system include preparation of quality manual, procedures, process work instructions, workmanship standards, drawing specifications and relevant quality records.

(*iii*) **Contract Review**

- This element states that the customer's requirements (the contract) should be formally reviewed to ensure that the supplier is capable in terms of both technical and organizational requirements.
- The records of those reviews should be properly maintained.

(*iv*) **Design Control**

- This element requires that the design process should be documented and planned correctly.
- Both the design inputs (like specifications) and the design outputs (like drawings) should be identified and documented.
- The supplier shall review the designs to ensure that the outputs meet the input requirements and that any changes to the designs are properly controlled.

(*v*) **Document Control**

- The ISO 9000 quality management system is totally documented system.
- This element explains the method of documentation, approval and issue of all quality documents.
- The various documents include quality manual, quality system procedures, work instructions, quality plans and quality records.

(*vi*) **Purchasing**

- This clause addresses issues relating to assessment of subcontractor, purchasing data, verification of purchased components, materials and procedures thereof are specified.
- The suppliers must have procedures for maintaining list of approved sub-contractors and suppliers, their assessment, inclusion of new sub-contractors, deleting sub-contracting, etc.
- This clause on purchasing / sub-contracting is applicable to raw materials, purchased components, sub-contracted components which are likely to affect the product.

(*vii*) **Purchaser Supplied Product (Control of Customer-Supplied Products)**

- In many situations the customer supplies various products. For example, in construction work, the customer may supply cement and steel. This clause explains how a system has to be laid down for inspection, storage and usage of customer supplied products.

- This clause also lays down the responsibility for preventing damage or loss and the same to be recorded and reported to the customer.

(*viii*) **Product Identification and Traceability**

- This clause lays down the requirement for the product or service to be correctly identified throughout the production process.
- Traceability means the method by which the item can be identified.

(*ix*) **Process Control**

- This clause specifies that the supplier shall identify and plan the production and installation processes which directly affect the quality.
- According to this clause, each process has to be performed under controlled conditions. Controlled conditions mean the following:
- Quality System Procedure (QSP) to describe how each process is carried out.
- Suitable production equipment and working environment.
- Compliance with relevant codes / standards and quality plans.
- Monitoring and control of specified process parameters and product characteristics.
- Approval of process as specified in quality system.
- Maintaining workmanship standards in terms of representative samples, sketches, photographs, details, write-ups, etc.
- Continuous monitoring to ensure continuing process capability.

(*x*) **Inspection and Testing**

- This clause explains how to lay down the system for inspection and testing at different stages: Receiving inspection and testing, in-process inspection and testing, and final inspection and testing. Records of all inspections and tests are to be maintained.
- Receiving inspection and testing: This is to ensure that product/material/service received from subcontractor/vendors conform to specifications laid down in the purchase order.
- In process inspection and testing: Process parameters and product characteristics are monitored/measured through in-process inspection and testing to ensure conformance.
- Final inspection and testing: This clause explains how system of final inspection and testing is implemented to ensure conformance to specifications before delivery to customer.

(*xi*) **Inspection, Measuring and Test Equipment (IMTE)**

This clause describes about the following points:

- Identifying the measurements to be made and the accuracy required.
- Selecting appropriate inspection, measuring and test equipments.
- Calibrating the measuring equipments and test devices.
- Maintaining calibration records for inspection, measuring and test equipments.

(*xii*) **Inspection and Test Status**

- This clause explains how the system should be laid down to indicate that the product has been inspected and tested and conforms or does not conform to specifications at various stages of production.

(*xiii*) **Control of Non-conforming Products**

- This clause lays down how action should be taken that does not conform to specifications.
- This control includes identification, documentation, evaluation, segregation and disposal of non-conforming product.
- Non-conformity is reviewed by specified authority to decide further action which could be rework, repair, and acceptance with concession.
- Record of reviews has to be maintained.
- This part of the standard is sometimes referred to as the calibration section.

(*xiv*) **Corrective and Preventive Action**

This clause explains the system for removing actual and potential non-conformities.

- Corrective action includes effective handling of customer complaints; investigation of the cause of non-conformity; and its removal.
- Prevention action is taken to ensure that non-conformity does not occur. This is done, by continuous study and analysis of various sources of information.

(*xv*) **Handling, Storage, Packaging, Preservation and Delivery**

- This clause explains how the supplier ensures that there is no degradation of quality of product due to handling, storage, preservation and delivery at different stages of production.
- This part of the standard is sometimes referred to as the housekeeping section.

(*xvi*) **Control of Quality Records**

- The records of the performance of the quality system (contract review, sub-contractor assessments, test records, calibration data, etc.) should be established and maintained.
- These records are essential for assessment of the effectiveness of the quality system by the internal/external certification audits and management reviews.

(*xvii*) **Internal Quality Audit**

- This clause describes the self-evaluation mechanism. These are carried out by the suppliers' own people trained for the purpose.
- These audits are used to verify the effectiveness of the quality system.
- The audit results should be documented and reported to the concerned managers to take any identified corrective actions.

(*xviii*) **Training**

- This clause describes how training needs of personnel are identified, organized, implemented and monitored.
- Appropriate records of all training should be maintained.

- Training pertains to professional training as well as training for maintenance and implementation of quality system.

(*xix*) **Servicing**

- This clause explains how servicing will be planned and executed wherever it is a specified requirement.
- Record of service provided should be maintained.

(*xx*) **Statistical Techniques**

- This clause describes that the organisation has to identify the most useful statistical techniques (such as Pareto analysis, Histograms, PERT, etc.) for its operations.

5.5.8 Implementation of Quality System (Steps to Registration)

Implementation of ISO 9000 quality management system in any organisation (Both manufacturing and services), generally requires the following steps.

Step 1: Top Management Commitment

- The most important step in implementing a quality stem is to get the full support of upper management.
- The top management must be willing to commit the resources necessary to achieve certification.

Step 2: Appoint the Management Representative

- The next step is the appointment of a management representative. The representative can be a member of the top management group.
- The management representative is responsible for coordinating the implementation and maintenance of the quality system. Also he is the contact person for all parties involved in the process, both internal and external.

Step 3: Awareness

- The next step is to create awareness about the ISO 9000 quality management system.
- Since the implementation of the quality system requires involvement of all members in the organisation, the members should understand the process and implications of ISO program.

Step 4: Appoint an Implementation Team

- Now the implementation team should be formed.
- This team should be drawn from all levels and areas of the organisation.
- The team should identify the quality management system processes and their sequence and interaction.

Step 5 : Training

- The implementation team, supervisors, and internal audit team should be trained.
- This activity can be accomplished through in-house training programs, seminars, workshops, etc.

Step 6 : Time Schedule

- This activity develops a time schedule for the implementation and registration of the system.
- This time frame will vary, depending on the size and type of organisation.

Step 7: Select Element Owners

- The implementation team selects owners for each of the system elements. Many of these owners will be members of the implementation team.
- Each owner has the option of selecting a team to assist in the process. Step

Step 8: Review the Present System

- A review of the present quality system should be performed.
- Copies of all the quality manuals, procedures, work instructions, and forms presently in use are obtained.
- This activity is a gap analysis and can be performed by the element owners and their teams or by an external consultant.

Step 9: Write the Documents

- Written quality policy and procedure manuals should be prepared.
- This documentation of work instructions should be done by the employee who performs the job.

Step 10 : Install the New System

- The policies, procedures, and work instructions should be integrated into the day-to-day workings of the organisation.
- Now the new system is installed.

Step 11 : Internal Audit

- An internal audit of the quality system should be conducted.
- This step ensures that the system is working effectively and to provide management with information for the comprehensive management review.

Step 12: Management Review

- The management review should be conducted in order to determine the effectiveness of the system in achieving the stated quality goals.

Step 13 : Preassessment

- The preassessment is an optional step. If a good job has been done on the previous steps, then preassessment is not necessary.

Step 14: Registration

- The registration activity includes: choosing a registrar, submitting an application, and conducting the registrar's system audit.
- While choosing a registrar, one should consider so many factors such as cost, lead time, and customer's acceptance of the registrar, the registrar's accreditation, and familiarity with the industry.
- The application for registration should also include supplying the registrar with the policy and procedure manuals for their review.
- The time involved in the registrar's system audit will vary depending on the size and complexity of the organisation and the number of auditors involved.

Step 15: Award of ISO 9000 Certificate

- After accepting the application and setting a time frame for registration, the registrar will review the quality system documentation.
- Based on the satisfactory report of the assessment team, license *i.e.*, ISO certificate will be granted to the organisation by ISO/BIS to use the certification mark in letter heads, quality certificates, etc.
- The certificate awarded is normally valid for 3 years. During the period of validity, surveillance audits are conducted to ensure that the document quality system is being effectively maintained.
- The surveillance audits will not be full audits but random checks of some elements to ensure that the system continues to function.

5.6 DOCUMENTATION OF QUALITY SYSTEM

5.6.1 Importance of Documentation

- It is understood that the proper documentation is the pre-requisite for implementing quality system.
- The documentation serves as a reference for the management, the staff and other agencies whose involvement is essential for implementation of the quality system.

Advantages of documented quality system

Documentations

(*a*) Serves as a reference;

(*b*) Brings about clarity of objectives and targets;

(*c*) Provides standardisation in work procedures;

(*d*) Brings about consistency in operations;

(*e*) Develops confidence amongst employees;

(*f*) Generates customer's confidence;

(*g*) Provides a basis for continuous improvement, etc.

Requirements of Documentation

The documents requires by most organisations are:

- Quality Policy Manual
- Quality System Procedures (QSPs)
- Work Instructions (WIs)
- Records/Formats/Forms

The above system documentation can be viewed as a hierarchy containing four levels as shown in Figure 5.1.

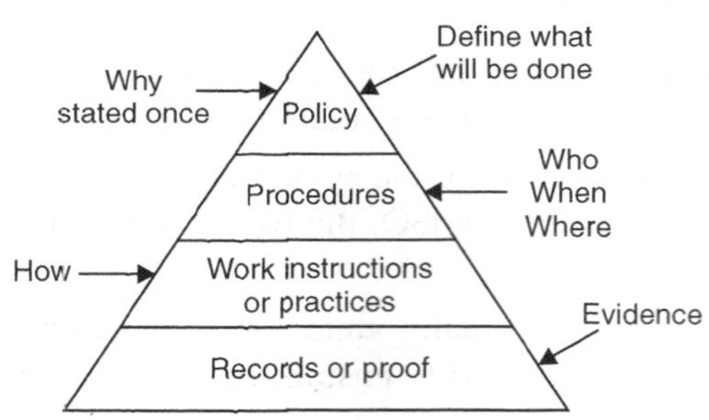

FIGURE 5.1 **Documentation Pyramid**

(*a*) **Quality Policy Manual:** Quality policy manual is the first level of documentation. This is the document that defines 'what will be done' and 'why'. The 'why' can be stated just once as a quality policy statement. This statement should be a short and simple definition of the organisation's quality intentions. The remainder of the policy manual addresses what will be done to comply with the standard being used. The policy manual communicates the quality policy and objectives of an organization. This manual is a living document. Because it reflects the current system being followed in the organisation.

(*b*) **Quality System Procedures (QSPs):** The second level of documentation is the quality procedures. These procedures describe the methods that will be used to implement and perform the stated policies. These procedures define who should perform specific tasks, when the task should be done, and where documentation will be made. These documents collectively define the organisation's operations from receiving an enquiry to delivering a completed product or service. These procedures are confidential documents of the organisation and therefore need not be revealed to outsiders.

(*c*) **Work Instructions (WIs):** This third level of documentation is generally company specific. It gives details of how individual work processes (for example, machining, welding, casting, etc.) are carried out within a company. Work instructions should also specify how the work should be done; who should undertake the work and what records are to be maintained. The work instructions may be in the form of a detailed drawing, recipe, routing sheet, specific job function, photograph, video, or simply a sample for comparison of conformity. The work instructions should be written by the employee who performs the task.

(*d*) **Records/Formats/Forms:** These provide evidence of activity having been performed in compliance with quality system procedure. Records may be forms that are filled out, a stamp of approval on a product, or a signature and date on some type of document. Records are used to provide traceability of actions taken on a specific product or batch of products.

5.6.2 Benefits of Documentation

The documentation of quality systems serves the following benefits:

- Documentation regularises the method of performing the day-to-day activities.
- It provides formats for standardising practices.
- It provides reference for assessing degree of enforcement in practice.
- It facilitates trouble shooting for tracing back on the processes.
- It demonstrates the ISO quality system certification.

5.7 QUALITY AUDITING

5.7.1 Meaning

Quality auditing should be carried out in order to verify whether a quality system is effective and suitable.

5.7.2 Definition of Quality Audit

A quality system audit is defined as "*A systematic and independent examination to determine whether quality activities and related results comply with planned arrangements, whether these arrangements are implemented effectively and whether these are suitable to achieve objectives*".

5.7.3 Features of Quality Audits

Following are the salient features about quality audits are:

- The quality audit typically applies to quality systems or elements such as processes, products or services. Such audits are often called 'quality system audits', 'process quality audits', 'product quality audits' and 'service quality audit' respectively.
- Quality audits are carried by staff that is not directly responsible in the areas being audited. But preferably auditors should work in cooperation with relevant personnel.
- Quality audit is an information gathering activity. It is not a police kind of activity.
- Quality audits may be conducted for internal or external purposes.
- They need not cover whole quality system, at once, but may cover elements of it.

5.7.4 Types of Audits

The general classification of audits is given below:

(*a*) **First party audit (or Internal audit):** This refers to an internal audit where the auditee is its own client, *i.e.*, audit is done by an organisation, working on itself.

(*b*) **Second party audit:** This refers to audit by one organisation on another organisation (auditee). This type of audit is normally done on a supplier by a customer.

(*c*) **Third party audit:** This refers to audit by an independent organisation on a supplier, for accreditation assessment purposes.

5.7.5 Objectives of Quality Audits/Need for Quality Audits

The objectives of quality audit programmes are:

- To determine the conformity or non-conformity of the quality system elements with regard to specified requirements.
- To determine the effectiveness of the implemented quality system in meeting specified quality objectives.
- To meet regulatory requirements, if applicable.
- To permit the listing of the audited organisation's quality system in a register for third party certification.
- To evaluate an organisation's own quality system against a quality system standard.

5.7.6 Stages of an Audit

There are four stages of auditing. They are:

- Audit planning,
- Audit performance,
- Audit reporting, and
- Audit follow-up.

Stage 1 : Audit Planning

The key elements in the audit planning stage are given below:

Audit schedules: It is a matrix of the timings, which details when each audit element is to be checked throughout the year.

Audit personnel: It refers to the appointment of an auditor.

Notification to the auditee: This is the formal and timely request by audit to auditee for making available all quality system documents relevant to the audit.

Preparation of checklist: This lists all specific questions to be asked during audit.

Stage 2 : Audit Performance

The key elements in the audit performance stage are given below:

Opening/entry meetings: Opening meeting is organised to initially brief the auditee about the scope of audit.

Audit process: Audit is run to schedule and should cover entire scope, as planned. Regular liaison meetings should be held.

Audit deficiencies: During auditing, clear and precise discrepancy reports are raised. All discrepancies should be based on sound and objective evidence.

Stage 3 : Audit Reporting

Audit reporting deals with the recording of any non-conformity and summarizing the audit findings.

The audit report may contain:

- Identification of the reference documents against which audit is conducted (*i.e.*, quality system standard), company's quality manual, etc.
- Observations of non-conformities.
- Corrective action requests.

Stage 4 : Audit Follow-up

The auditor is responsible only for identifying the non-conformity. But the auditee is responsible for determining and initiating corrective action needed to correct a non conformity.

Corrective action and subsequent follow-up should be completed within a time period agreed to by the client and the auditee in consultation with the auditing organisation. These four stages complete the ISO 9000 quality system audit.

5.8 QUALITY SYSTEM 9000(QS 9000)—AUTOMOTIVE QUALITY MANAGEMENT SYSTEMS

5.8.1 Introduction to QS 9000

QS 9000 is a set of quality system requirements recently adopted by members of the automotive industry. QS 9000 was proposed by Chrysler, Ford and General Motors in 1994. QS 9000 is harmonization of Chrysler's Supplier Quality Assurance Manual, Ford's Q-101 Quality System Standard and General Motor's NAO Targets for Excellence.

QS 9000 focuses on helping automotive suppliers to ensure that they are meeting/exceeding automotive customer requirements. QS 9000 is now being replaced by a newer related standard called ISO/TS 16949. TS 16949 contain all of ISO 9000, QS 9000 and many European standards.

5.8.2 Objectives of QS 9000

The objective of QS 9000 is to develop fundamental quality systems based on continuous improvement, direct prevention, reduction of variation and waste elimination in the automobiles supply chain.

5.8.3 Application of QS 9000

QS 9000 can be applied to all internal and external suppliers of

- Production materials,
- Production or service parts, and
- Heat treating, painting, plating or finishing services.

5.8.4 Structure of QS 9000

QS 9000 standards can be divided into three sections. They are:

- ***Section I:*** *ISO 9000 Based Requirements*
- ***Section II:*** *Automotive Sector Specific Requirements*
- ***Section III:*** *Customer Specific Requirements*

(*a*) **Section I: ISO 9000 Based Requirements:** The Section I requirements includes the exact text of ISO 9001 with the addition of automotive/heavy trucking requirements.

(*b*) **Section II: Automotive Sector Specific Requirements:**

- This section includes common requirements for all automotive supplies, agreed by the 'Big three' (*i.e.*, Chryster, Ford Motor, and General Motors).
- The sector specific requirements are:
- Production - Part Approved Process (P-PAP),
- Continuous improvement, and
- Manufacturing capabilities (such as facilities planning, mistake proofing, and tooling management).

(*c*) **Section III : Customer Specific Requirements:** This section deals with the specific requirements of each customer over and above the requirements specified in Section II.

5.8.5 Documents Required for QS 9000 Programme

The minimum seven documents required for the QS 9000 program are:

(*a*) QS 9000 quality system requirements,

(*b*) Advanced Product Quality Planning (APQP) and control plan,

(*c*) Failure Mode and Effects Analysis (FMEA),
(*d*) Measurement system analysis,
(*e*) Fundamental statistical process control,
(*f*) Production Part Approval Process (PPAP) manual, and
(*g*) Quality System Assessment (QSA) manual.

5.9 ISO 14000: ENVIRONMENTAL MANAGEMENT SYSTEM STANDARDS

5.9.1 ISO 14000—Introduction

After the success of the ISO 9000 series of quality standards, the International Organization for Standards (ISO) has developed a compressive set of standards for environmental management (which is known as ISO 14000 series) in 1992. The ISO 14000 standards are a set of norms for Environmental Management System (EMS) either at organisation and process level or product level.

The series of ISO 14000 standards are designed to cover

- Environmental management systems,
- Environmental auditing,
- Environmental performance evaluation,
- Life-cycle assessment, and
- Environmental aspects in product standards.

5.9.2 Importance of ISO 14000 Standards

- The ISO 14000 standards bring a world-wide focus to the environment, encouraging a cleaner, safer, healthier world for all. The existence of the standards allows organisations to focus environmental efforts against internationally accepted criteria.
- At present many countries and regional groupings are generating their own requirements for environmental issues and these vary between the groups. A single standard will ensure that there are no conflicts between regional interpretations of good environmental practice.
- Nowadays, companies require environmental management certification to compete in the global marketplace. So the ISO 14000 registration may become the primary requirement for doing business in many regions or industries.

5.9.3 ISO 14000 Series of Standards

The entire ISO 14000 series can be divided into two areas. They are:

(*a*) Organization evaluation standards, and
(*b*) Product evaluation standards.

In addition, ISO 14050 covers terms and definitions that are common to both organisation and product areas.

(*a*) **Organization Evaluation Standards:** The various organization evaluation standards are depicted in the figure.

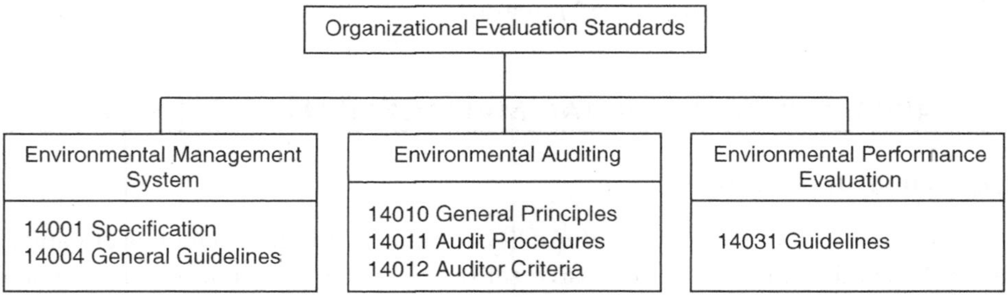

As the above figure, organization evaluation standards consists of the following three categories:

(*i*) Environmental Management System,

(*ii*) Environmental Auditing (EA), and

(*iii*) Environmental Performance Evaluation (EPE).

Following table gives the description about the various organisation evaluation standards.

Designation	Publication	Title	Description
ISO14001: 1996	1996	Environmental Management Systems - Specifications with Guidance for Use	It gives the elements that organisations are required to conform to get registration certificate.
ISO14004: 1996	1996	Environmental Management Systems - Guidelines on Principles, Systems and Supporting Techniques	It provides supplementary material. It is only for information and not used for registration.
ISO 14010: 1996	1996	Guidelines for Environmental Auditing - General Principles on Environmental Auditing	It provides information for internal or external auditing.
ISO 14011: 1996	1996	Guidelines for Environmental Auditing - Audit Procedures - Auditing of Environmental Management Systems	It provides information on how to plan and conduct an audit.
ISO 14012: 1996	1996	Guidelines for Environmental Auditing-Qualification Criteria for Environmental Auditors.	It covers information on auditor qualification, training, and personal attributes and skills.
ISO 14031: 1999	1999	Guidelines on Environmental Performance Evaluation	It helps the organisation to meet the requirements of ISO 14001, monitoring, and measuring.

(*b*) **Product Evaluation Standards:** The various product evaluation standards are shown in the chart.

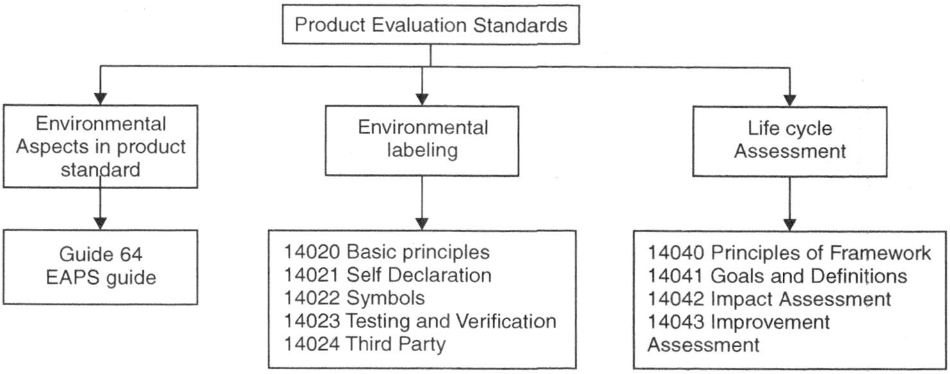

Product Evaluation Standards consists of the following three categories:

- Environmental Aspects in Product Standards (EAPS),
- Environmental Labels and Declarations (ELD), and
- Life Cycle Assessment (LCA).

Following table gives the description about the various product evaluation standards.

Designation	Publication	Title	Description
ISO Guide 64: 1997	1997	Environmental Aspects in Product Standards.	It is designed to help writers to develop product standards.
ISO 14020: 2000	2000	Labels and Declarations - Environmental Basic Principles for All Environmental Labeling	It provides guidance on the goals and principles that should be used in all labeling Programs.
ISO 14021: 1999	1999	Environmental Labels and Declarations - Self-Declaration of Environmental claims: Terms and Conditions	It ensures that this type of labeling is accurate, verifiable, and not deceptive.
ISO 14022: 1999	1999	Environmental Labels and Declarations - Symbols	It provides a standard set of symbols for use by organisations.
ISO 14023:1999	1999	Environmental Labels and Declarations - Testing and Verification Methodologies.	It provides information on the appropriate methods to use to confirm the guidelines of the product.
ISO 14024: 1999	1999	Environmental Labels and Declarations - Practitioner Programs : Guiding Principles, Practices, and Certification Procedures for Multiple Criteria Programs.	It establishes criteria for third party labeling or seal programs.

(Contd...)

ISO 14040: 1997	1997	Life Cycle Assessment - Principles and Framework	It provides an overview of the practice, applications limitations of life cycle assessment.
ISO 14041 : 1998	1998	Life Cycle Assessment - Goals and Definition / Scope and Inventory Analysis	It provides guidelines for the preparation, conduct, and critical review of the life cycle inventory analysis.
ISO 14042 : 2000	2000	Life Cycle Assessment - Impact Assessment	It is intended to use the results of the inventory analysis to evaluate the significance of potential environmental impacts.
ISO 14043:2000	2000	Life Cycle Assessment - Improvement Assessment	It provides information improve the total environmental performance of a product system.

5.9.4 Terminologies used in ISO 14000 Standards

In order to understand the concept and requirements of ISO 14000, one should be familiar with the following terms:

(*a*) **Environment:** It is defined as the global surroundings in which an organisation operates and includes air, water, land, natural resources, flora, fauna, humans, and their interaction.

(*b*) **Environmental aspect:** It is defined as an element of an organisation's activities, products, or services that can interact with the environment. Examples are waste water discharge, air emissions, and energy usage.

(*c*) **Environmental impact:** It is defined as any change, whether adverse or beneficial, wholly or partially resulting from an organisation's activities, products, or services. Examples are impact on water supply and soil erosion.

(*d*) **Environmental objective:** It is an overall environmental goal, arising from the policy statement that an organisation sets for itself. For example, an objective could be to control the carbon percentage of the outlet stroke.

(*e*) **Environmental target:** It is a detailed performance requirement and should be quantified when practical. For example, say, the carbon percentage of the outlet smoke' should be controlled between 2% and 3%.

5.9.5 Requirements of ISO 14000 or Major Elements of EMS Standards

The major elements of an EMS standard are:

- General requirements,
- Environmental policy,
- Environmental aspects,

- Legal aspects,
- Objectives and targets,
- Environmental management programme,
- Structure and responsibility,
- Training, awareness and competency,
- Communication,
- Environmental management system documentation,
- Document control,
- Operational control,
- Emergency preparedness and response,
- Monitoring and measuring,
- Non-conformance and corrective and preventive action,
- Records,
- EMS audit, and
- Management review.

(*i*) **General Requirements:** This clause addresses the general requirements of ISO 14000 to the organisations. This element requires that the organisation should establish and maintain an environmental management system (EMS). The EMS includes policy, planning, implementation and operation, checking and corrective action, and management review. This element also insists the organisation to include a brief description of the company.

(*ii*) **Environmental Policy:** This clause explains the contents to be included in the environmental policy. The environmental policy should address the following issues:

- Management commitment to continual improvement,
- Prevention of pollution,
- Compliance with environment laws and regulation, cooperation with public authorities,
- Creating a framework for setting objectives,
- Communication requirements with shareholders, and
- Education and training for environment.

(*iii*) **Environmental Aspects:** This clause explains about the environmental aspects and its relationship with the environmental impacts. The process of identification of environmental aspects is somewhat similar to FMEA analysis. These aspects that relate to significant impacts shall be considered in setting objectives.

(*iv*) **Legal Aspects:** This clause explains the organisation to have a procedure to identify and have access to all legal requirements to which it subscribes. Legal requirements include industry code of practice, contracts, agreement with public authorities, non-regulatory guidelines, and governmental legislative and regulatory action. However the organisations need to identify only those requirements that are applicable to the environmental aspects of its activities, products, and services.

(*v*) **Objectives and Targets:** This element describes the organisation to establish and maintain the objectives and targets at each relevant function and level.

(*vi*) **Environmental Management Programme:** This clause details the organisation to establish and maintain a program for achieving the objectives and targets. The program shall include designation of the responsible function, team, or individual and a timeframe for achievement.

(*vii*) **Structure and Responsibility:** This element addresses the roles, responsibilities, and authorities of all personnel affecting the EMS. The management should provide the resources in terms of people, technology, and money to implement and maintain an effective system that achieves its objectives.

(*viii*) **Training, Awareness, and Competency:** This clause details the training needs to be evaluated, to ensure the system effectiveness. The two types of training are: general awareness and job competency.

General awareness includes the importance of conformance to the EMS, the relationship of significant environmental impacts to the employees' work activities, employee roles and responsibilities, and potential consequences of failing to follow specific operating procedures.

(*ix*) **Communication:** This element describes the procedures to be established and maintained for communication (both internal and external) with all stakeholders.

(*x*) **Environmental Management System Documentation:** This element requires that information be established and maintained to describe the core elements of the system and their interaction and provide direction to applicable related documents.

(*xi*) **Document Control :** This element requires that procedures be established and maintained to control all EMS documents. Examples are blueprints, test procedures, work instructions, and the EMS manual.

The purpose of document control is to ensure that appropriate and current issues of documents are in place at all locations. The four levels of documentation are: policy level, procedure level, practice level, and proof level.

(*xii*) **Operational Control:** This element aligns operations and activities with the identified significant environmental aspects, environmental policy, and environmental objectives and targets.

(*xiii*) **Emergency Preparedness and Response:** This element describes the procedures to identify and respond to potential accidents and emergency situations. The procedures should also prevent the environmental impact of these accidents and emergency situations.

(*xiv*) **Monitoring and Measuring:** This element requires that the organisation to monitor and measure the key characteristic, of its objectives and activities in order to assess its performance in meeting environmental operations and targets. Procedures should be in place to control, regularly calibrate, maintain and record all EMS equipment. Procedures are also required to periodically evaluate compliance to relevant regulations.

(*xv*) **Non-conformance and Corrective and Preventive Action:** This clause describes the procedures to define responsibility and authority for:

- handling and investigating non-conformance,
- taking action to minimise any impacts, and
- initiating corrective and preventive action.

(*xvi*) **Records:** This system requires procedures for the identification, maintenance, and disposition of environmental records. Environmental records include training, audits, equipment calibration and reviews. Records should be legible, identifiable, and traceable to the activity, product or service.

(*xvii*) **EMS Audit:** The purpose of EMS audit is to ensure that the EMS conforms to plans. Audit procedures should cover the scope, frequency and methodologies, and responsibilities and requirements for conducting audits and reporting results.

Internal or self-audit and external audit information should be forwarded to the top management to assist in the management review process.

(xviii) **Management Review:** The intent of this clause is to involve top management in the EMS continuous improvement process. Management should evaluate the feedback data and make improvements to the system.

5.9.6 Environmental Management System Model (Concept of ISO 14000)

ISO 14000 series of standards can be applicable to all types and sizes of organisations and to accommodate diverse geographical, cultural, and social conditions. The basic approach to Environmental Management System (EMS) is depicted in Figure. EMS approach is based on PDCA (Plan, Do, Check and Act) cycle.

The EMS model consists of the following five stages:

- **Stage 1:** Environmental Policy (EP)
- **Stage 2:** Planning
- **Stage 3:** Implementation and Operation
- **Stage 4:** Checking and Corrective Action
- **Stage 5:** Management Review

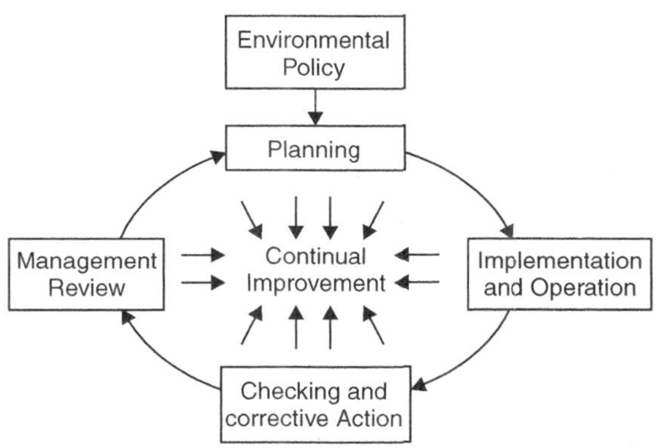

FIGURE 5.2 **Environmental Management System Model**

Stage 1: Environmental Policy (EP)

The environmental policy should address the following issues:

- Management commitment to continual improvement, *i.e.*, core values and beliefs in making environment policy;
- Prevention of pollution;
- Compliance with environment laws and regulation, cooperation with public authorities;
- Creating a framework for setting objectives;
- Communication requirements with shareholders; and
- Education and training for environment.

The management should ensure that the policy is implemented and carried out.

Stage 2: Planning

- This planning stage contains four elements such as environmental aspects, legal and other requirements, objectives and targets, and environmental management program(s).
- The environmental aspects of an organisation's activities, products, and services should be identified in order to determine the environmental impact.
- The organisation should identify and have access to all legal and other requirements to which it subscribes.
- The organisation should establish and maintain the objectives and targets at each relevant function and level.
- The organisation should establish and maintain a program(s) for achieving the objectives and targets.

Stage 3: Implementation and Operation

- This stage contains seven elements such as structure and responsibility; training, awareness and competency; communication; EMS documentation; document control; operational control; and emergency preparedness and response.
- Roles, responsibilities, and authorities should be defined, documented, and communicated for all personnel affecting the EMS.
- Training needs should be evaluated on a regular basis to ensure their effectiveness.
- The EMS implementation requires proper communication with all stakeholders.
- The organisation should establish and maintain information, in paper or electronic form, to describe the core elements of the system.
- Procedures should be established and maintained to control all EMS documents.
- Procedures should be formed to identify and respond to potential accidents and emergency situations.

Stage 4: Checking and Corrective Action

- This stage contains four elements such as monitoring and measuring; non-conformance and corrective and preventive action; records; and EMS audit.

- The organisation should monitor and measure the key characteristics of its objectives and activities in order to assess its performance in meeting environmental operations and targets.
- Procedures should be established to define responsibility and authority for (*i*) handling and investigating non-conformance; and (*ii*) initiating corrective and preventive action.
- The organisation should establish procedures for the identification, maintenance, and disposition of environmental records such 'as training, audits, equipment calibration, and reviews.
- EMS audit should be carried out to ensure that the EMS conforms to plans.

Stage 5 : Management Review

- Management should review and revise the system in order to ensure the continuing suitability, adequacy, and effectiveness of the EMS.
- The management must evaluate the feedback data and make improvements to the systems.

Thus EMS implementation is based on PDCA cycle.

5.9.7 Benefits of ISO 14000

The benefits of implementing ISO 14000 quality system can be viewed in two categories:

- Global benefits, and
- Organizational benefits.

Global benefits: The three major global benefits of implementing ISO 14000 are:

- To facilitate trade and remove trade barriers,
- To improve environmental performance of planet earth, and
- To build consensus that there is a need for environmental management and a common terminology for EMS.

Organisation benefits: Significant benefits have been observed in the organisation in the following ways:

- Satisfying customer requirements.
- Assuring customers of a commitment to environmental management.
- Maintaining a good relationship with public/community/society.
- Improving access to capital by improving the confidence of the investors.
- Satisfying insurance criteria and obtaining insurance at reasonable cost.
- Increasing market share that results from a competitive advantage.
- Reducing incidents that result in liability.
- Facilitating the attainment of permits and authorization.
- Conserving input resources.
- Improving industry/government relations.
- Improving teamwork.

INDEX

F

G

H

I

J

K

L

M

N

O

P

Q

R

S

T

V

W